# *Hidden Gems*
## *of*
# THE BLACK COUNTRY

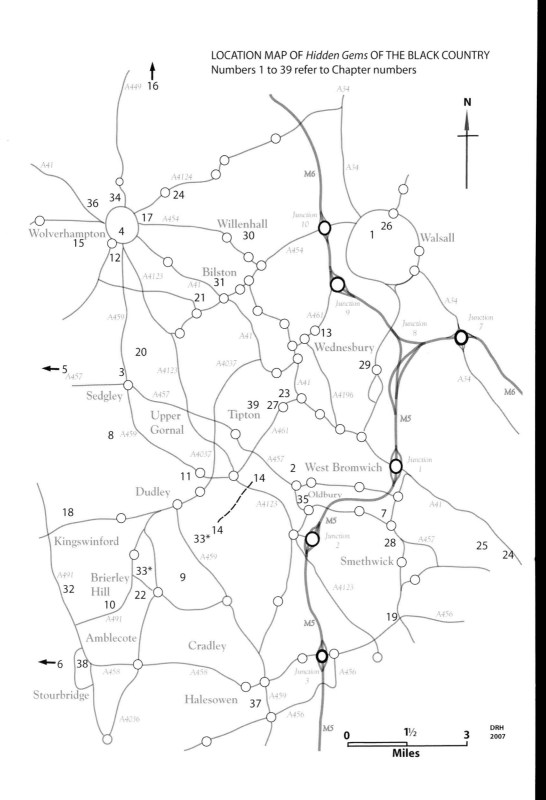

LOCATION MAP OF *Hidden Gems* OF THE BLACK COUNTRY
Numbers 1 to 39 refer to Chapter numbers

# *Hidden Gems*
# *of*
# THE BLACK COUNTRY

David Harvey and Eric Richardson

**SLP**

Silver Link Publishing Ltd

# *Acknowledgements*

This book would not have been possible without the portfolio of delightful pen and ink sketches drawn over a 30-year period by Eric Richardson, without whose enthusiasm this volume could not have been completed.

Special thanks are due to Peter Drake of the Local Studies Department of the Birmingham Central Reference Library, who allowed me access to their photographic archive. Expert advice and photographs came from Terry Daniels, whose photographs and background information has greatly improved the chapter on Oldbury. Terry Price provided both a lovely photograph and background to St Peter's Church, Great Bridge. We are very grateful to John Hughes, who has provided a number of historic photographs from the Wolverhampton area that have enhanced this book.

One of the most important facets in book production is that of the publisher. Peter Townsend of Silver Link Publishing has backed this uniquely styled project, and has managed to crowbar the writer's verbosity into a tiny space and yet produce an imaginative and artistic page layout.

Stan Hill of the Black Country Society has kindly proofread and commented upon the historical accuracy of the book, which has the drawings of a Welshman and the words of someone from that other place … er … Birmingham! Finally there has to be a great big thank you to Nancy Richardson who proofread several drafts of the text, and to my wife Diana, who as well as proofreading the text and suggesting ways out of many a linguistic cul-de-sac also accompanied me on a number of my photographic excursions around the Black Country.

David Harvey, Dudley

*Title page* CRADLEY HEATH: Chain maker's workshop in 1907
*Title page (insets)* CRADLEY HEATH: Women stacking newly fired bricks. Two Black

Country 'wenches' working at a chain maker's shop in about 1907

First published in 2007

British Library Cataloguing in Publication Data

Printed and bound in the Czech Republic

A catalogue record for this book is available from the British Library.
ISBN 978 1 85794 261 3

Silver Link Publishing Ltd
The Trundle
Ringstead Road
Great Addington
Kettering
Northants NN14 4BW

Tel/Fax: 01536 330588
email: sales@nostalgiacollection.com
Website: www.nostalgiacollection.com

# Contents

# *Preface*

This book offers the reader a vignette of the Black Country region by taking a fairly random look at some of the more interesting historical sites. The deliberately idiosyncratic layout of the book is intended to capture some feel of the diversity and almost parochial nature of the Black Country. The isolated locations featured are scattered around the area and the book cover a wide variety of topics. Churches, statues, houses, canals and railways, public houses, heritage areas and industrial sites are included, not to show the whole of the Black Country but to point the reader towards some of its hidden and not so hidden gems.

The book uses the excellent drawings of Eric Richardson, historic photographs and present-day photographs to show how the 39 locations have altered over time. The sheer awfulness of the industrial 19th century contrasts with the beauty of houses that possess an interesting history, while churches with 'a certain something' about them are also included. Striking feats of engineering stand as monuments to the pioneering work born out of entrepreneurial necessity and remain as a legacy to the industrial greatness that helped to make the Black Country one of the United Kingdom's most prosperous areas, particularly in the 19th century. Many of the places illustrated date from this period of greatness and reveal a wide diversity of style, function and form. Sadly, many buildings, canal and railway routes, with their frequently amazing achievements of engineering, and primary and heavy industries have, of course, disappeared, but just occasionally something outstanding has survived, and some of these 'hidden gems' are found here.

So what constitutes a 'hidden gem'? I suppose that what is a 'gem' to one person is a monstrosity to another, while the people who live next to one of these supposedly 'hidden' places might well wonder what all the fuss is about! It therefore follows that this book is a combined, yet subjective look by the author and the artist as to what they considered to be 'gems', some of which are well known and others genuinely hidden. It was what to leave out rather than what to include that made the task of selecting the featured places most difficult. With about 100 drawings to choose from, the aim with those examples that were eventually chosen to explore in more detail was to show the diversity and range of what there is to look at in the Black Country. This is no gazetteer, nor is it a definitive journey around the region, but rather a random way of showing the 'hidden gems' worth visiting and exploring, while at the same time attempting to cover the area geographically, historically, socially, industrially, ecclesiastically and domestically.   We hope you enjoy the contrasting chapters and trust that they might inspire you to go and look at the locations featured – and perhaps lead you to find some more 'special' places of your own. Good hunting!

# Introduction:
## What is the Black Country?

Defining the Black Country as a geographic area is an extremely difficult task as it is a very imprecise area. Beyond it are rural Staffordshire, Shropshire and Worcestershire to the north, west and south, while to the east lies the old arch-enemy of Birmingham. The symbiotic relationship between Birmingham and the Black Country has produced two very different societies. While the outsider sees only 'Brummies', to the man or woman from Dudley or Willenhall or Cradley Heath that label is an insult – they have their own distinctive sense of geography, history and culture. To call someone from the Black Country a 'Brummie' is like showing a red rag to a bull!

The area has at its heart the ancient fortified town of Dudley, but today is organised through the Metropolitan Boroughs of Walsall, Wolverhampton, Dudley and Sandwell. Sandwell is, alas, not even a place, but for administration purposes this name was chosen to include West Bromwich, Wednesbury, Oldbury and Tipton, as well as what was briefly known as Warley, which included Smethwick and Rowley Regis. Lost in the local government re-organisations of 1966 and 1974 were the southern and western towns of Stourbridge, Halesowen and Brierley Hill, together with Coseley and Sedgley, which are now part of Dudley, while in the north-east Walsall acquired Darlaston and Willenhall. Wolverhampton has absorbed Wednesfield, Tettenhall and Bilston. It was as though someone in central government wanted simply to get rid of the area and by so doing destroy its heritage. Well, it has failed! The Black Country is alive and well, and although many places have two postal addresses such as 'Pleck, Walsall', the local residents – even those born after 1974 – don't say that they come from Sandwell when they go along to the highest football league ground in the United Kingdom and cheer on the 'Baggies' (West Bromwich Albion, to those who don't follow football).

Certainly the Black Country was based in part on the now largely unworked South Staffordshire coalfield; within, and adjacent to, this large area were huge reserves of iron ore, limestone, clay and sand. The South Staffordshire coalfield's Thick Coal seams were up to 30 feet thick, though this was only one of eight different coal seams, which were given names such as the Heathen Coal, Stinking Coal and Fireclay Coal. Open-cast mining took place in the north-east of the Black Country, while in the Hamstead and Sandwell areas shafts were sunk to between 1,200 and 1,800 feet. There were many other types of coal mining, from the simple one-man bell pits to the slightly larger and deeper gin pits, as shown in the accompanying 19th-century photograph

All the primary extractive industries were extensively worked to serve the iron foundries and other secondary processing industries across the region, while the localised glass industry around Stourbridge grew up because of the

Above UPPER GORNAL: A typical 'gin pit'
mine of which there were hundreds around the
Black Country

abundant supplies of high-quality fireclay
that the Huguenot glass-makers needed
to line their kilns. There were so many
furnaces belching out smoke and flames,
as well as the dependence on the coal
reserves, that the area became known as
the 'Black Country' at a time when the
emerging heavy industries enabled the
area to become one of the first cradles of
the Industrial Revolution anywhere in
the world. Other industries developed
in the area that were independent of
the iron industry, including the saddlery
trade in Walsall, the spinning of carpet
yarn in Wolverhampton and wool cloth
in Stourbridge, as well as the famous
glassware industry brought to the town by
Lorraine refugees from France in the late
17th century.

After the early development of the
domestic nails, chain, bolts and screw
industries, ironmasters across the area
became extremely powerful men with
inventive minds who, within 50 years,
changed the one-man, hand-fired furnace
into a mechanical fully integrated blast
furnace. Iron was finished as plate, sheet,
bar, rod, strip, hoop and section, some of
which were impossible to make without
the improvements to the Newcomen

stationary steam engine
developed by James Watt
in 1769 at the Soho
Manufactory in Hockley.

The huge expansion of
industry led to the need
to export the products,
but the rivers of the West
Midlands were landlocked
and unnavigable. As a
result canal development,
which was begun in the
area in 1766 by the pioneer canal-builder
James Brindley, rapidly took hold so
that by November 1769 Birmingham,
Wednesbury and Wolverhampton were
all linked by the Birmingham Canal and
the price of coal halved overnight. The
Staffordshire-Worcestershire Canal was
completed by 1772, joining the River
Severn at Stourport, and the Birmingham
Canal linked with it at Autherley, which
now connected Birmingham and the
Black Country with the River Severn
ports. Thus, by the end of that century
most of the major furnaces had their
own canal basin or arm, Birmingham
had become 'the City of 1000 and one
trades', and the Black Country was the
growing 'hardware' centre. Unusually, the
canal system continued to develop, so it
was as late as 1855 when a third tunnel
was opened linking the Birmingham and
the Stour Navigations, known as the
Netherton Tunnel, beneath the central
ridge of the South Staffordshire coalfield.

A second method of transport, the
railway, came into the Black Country
when the Grand Junction Railway opened
its line, mainly for passenger use, on 4 July
1837 between Vauxhall in Birmingham
and Wolverhampton by way of the River
Tame Valley through Perry Barr, Bescot,
Willenhall and Wolverhampton. By
the early 1840s there developed a bitter

struggle between the London & North Western Railway and the 'Broad Gauge' lines of the Great Western Railway to capture the Black Country trade. With the arrival of the Midland Railway and the Oxford, Worcester & Wolverhampton Railway from the south-west in the 1850s, the 'Grand Cross' pattern developed, with main lines running from the south-west to the north-east and from the south-east to the north-west, even in some cases following the land occupied by the Birmingham Canal Navigations, whose Board had cleverly become major shareholders in the faster and more flexible railway companies. By the 1870s the Black Country was criss-crossed with main-line railways, branch lines, spurs into the larger foundries and factories, and mineral railways, many of which survived the demise of the coal and iron and steel industries until the savage cutbacks of the Beeching Plan in 1963.

By the 1850s and for the next decade the Black Country iron trade was at its peak, with the Corngreaves site in Cradley Heath being one of the most important iron-producing areas. Coupled with the use of Bessemer's acid converter process to make mild steel, large steel-making sites were developed at Wednesbury, Bilston and Brierley Hill. This was a period of prosperity in the area – at least for the industrialists. The ordinary worker, meanwhile, led a desperately hard life. The accompanying frontispiece photograph of the two young female Cradley Heath chain-makers in about 1907 shows this all too well. Just look at them – still young, still quite attractive, but already showing the signs of being worn out by their work. The woman behind the barred windows of her little chain shop looks more like a prisoner than a chain worker. What you don't see in another photograph taken inside the

forge is the woman's little urchin of a girl aged about three, sitting on a workbench surrounded with coal and waste metal. Pitiful and yet one hundred years ago still quite common. Pig iron production in the area reached its peak in 1865, and from about that time the coal industry began to contract in the Black Country so that by 1900 coal production was half what it had been 35 years earlier.

Traditional primary industry was dying, and at the end of the 19th century the emergence of the manufacturing of highly finished or highly composite products began. The result was that individual settlements developed their own, quite distinct industries. The list is endless, but examples are Willenhall, which became the centre of the lock industry, and Darlaston, which specialised in guns. Smethwick had Chance Brothers' world famous glassworks, while West Bromwich, with Salters, was the centre of the spring and weighing equipment industry. Oldbury became famous for the steel tube industry of Accles & Pollock, and in nearby Smethwick, the Birmingham Railway Carriage & Wagon Company was set up in 1864 and eventually constructed not just railway rolling-stock, but also Diesel locomotives, bus bodies and wartime tanks. Meanwhile Wolverhampton had the Great Western Railway's locomotive construction works, which was second only to Swindon, while the motor industry, with Sunbeam, Rudge, AJS, Clyno, Star and Guy Motors, as well as Villiers motor cycle engines and Henry Meadows car and commercial engine manufacturers, thrived throughout the first half of the 20th century.

What was unusual about the area was that the Black Country, as well as having its obvious larger towns, had countless numbers of smaller hamlets and villages at the time of the change-over from agriculture to industry in the mid-18th century. As a result of this, each one of these settlements developed its own fiercely independent trades and industries, traditions and culture, and even local dialect. Lost in the mists of time, for instance, is the never-ending feud between the inhabitants of Darlaston and Wednesbury. The Gornal area, near Dudley, had an isolated collection of settlements and became famous for its local sand as well as selling imported salt from Droitwich across the whole of the Black Country. The local topography around the Gornals precluded it from having any links either to the canal or railway systems, so it developed its own culture, dialect and sense of humour. It was in Gornal that the countless 'Aynuck and Ayli' stories, with their benignly acid Black Country sense of humour, developed, while it was always said that, between Upper Gornal, through Ruiton into Lower Gornal and down the hill to Gornal Wood, there were more public houses per square mile than anywhere else in Britain.

Indeed, until the all-pervasive Estuarine television language began to take its toll, the differences in the dialects of the West Midlands' Black Country accent were distinguishable almost between one street and another. Certainly someone from Wolverhampton might have found the speech of someone from Lye at least awkward to understand. Yet the Black Country accent and dialect is probably the nearest in Britain to the Old English of Geoffrey Chaucer, and is quite distinct from the 'Brummie' accent of Birmingham.

Looking at a 21st-century Ordnance Survey map, the continuous urban area radiating to the west of Birmingham belies the variations that have managed to survive to the present day. Where there are only road signs to let the motorist know that he is leaving, for instance, Netherton and passing on his way to Old Hill before reaching Cradley Heath, these do not account for the independence of each of these places. Local government re-organisations in both 1966 and 1974 did not kill the unique qualities of the individual places in the Black Country, which to an outsider were not noticeable.

The Black Country is therefore a far more complex, independent, proud and diverse area than one would perhaps first imagine. Despite the economic ravages caused by the decline of heavy industry, to the point where no youngster today could possibly understand why the area was originally called the 'Black Country', there are still places where remnants of a medieval agricultural way of life and industrial archaeology collide with the present day. It is this juxtaposition of events, people, buildings and places that makes this strangely ill-defined place so interesting and unique.

*Below* **NETHERTON**    **Chain makers at Noah Hingley Ltd circa 1910.**

# 1. Sister Dora's Statue, The Bridge, Walsall

DOROTHY WYNDLOW PATTISON – SISTER DORA WAS BORN ON 16TH JANUARY, 1832. SHE CAME TO WALSALL IN 1865 AND FOR THE FOLLOWING THIRTEEN YEARS WORKED CEASELESSLY TO ESTABLISH A PROFESSIONAL MEDICAL SERVICE IN THE TOWN. HER GREAT DEVOTION TO THE WORKING PEOPLE OF WALSALL EARNED HER WIDESPREAD RESPECT. WHEN SHE DIED IN 1878 THOUSANDS MOURNED HER AND LATER SHE BECAME THE COUNTRY'S FIRST WOMAN, OTHER THAN A MEMBER OF THE ROYAL FAMILY, TO BE COMMEMORATED BY A STATUE.

A 'hidden gem' today largely unnoticed in the middle of the busy Walsall town centre is the statue of Sister Dora that stands at The Bridge. The drawing of the statue shows a somewhat demure lady wearing clothes typical of a nurse practising her profession in the middle years of the Victorian period. Yet the story of the lady in question makes one realise what a heroine of the town she actually was.

Dorothy Wyndlow Pattison was born in 1832 and, after joining the Sisterhood of the Good Samaritans in 1864, moved to Walsall as a nurse during the following year, although the statue's inscription states that it was 1866. The London & Midland Bank, on the corner of the distant Lichfield Street, was the former premises of the Walsall Observer newspaper, and had been built on the site of where Sister Pattison worked in a couple of houses that served as a cottage hospital for the town. It was from these small premises that through the smallpox epidemics that plagued the town between 1868 and 1869 she began a period of selfless devotion to the patients that were brought to her, working almost single-handed to nurse her contagious charges. In 1871 Sister Dora, in recognition of 'her tender deeds and patient nursings to many of themselves', was presented with a pony and carriage by the employees of the London & North Western Railway. Such was the railway's veneration of the famous nurse that they named 'Whitworth Class' 2-4-0 express locomotive No 2158 Sister Dora.

After years of campaigning, Sister Pattison's efforts were rewarded when the General Hospital at the Mount in Wednesbury Road was opened in 1878, almost in sight of the old cottage hospital at The Bridge. Alas, by this time Sister Dora was a broken woman, having contracted many of the diseases that came through the doors of her original hospital. She died on Christmas Eve 1878, having been too ill to attend the opening ceremony. Her statue, in its original white marble form, was unveiled on 11 October 1886 in memory of her, and the esteem in which she was held was such that this was the first statue in the country erected to commemorate a female 'commoner'. In 1957 the statue was replaced with one cast in bronze, as the original had weathered badly due to pollution, but it retained the descriptive bronze dedication set into the marble base.

*Below:* The replacement 'four-faced liar' town centre timepiece has now been located away from Sister Dora's statue on the corner of Bridge Street and St Paul's Street. Beyond the impressive cupola-topped corner premises of the HSBC bank and partly masked by the clock is the Imperial Building, which dates from 1899. Most of the premises on this north side of Bridge Street date from the same decade as the original statue of Sister Dora.

*Opposite top:* On 30 April 2005 pedestrians rush across the exposed open space at The Bridge while an Andean flute duo prepare to play their bamboo instruments beneath the relocated statue of Sister Dora, which was moved from its original site at the bottom of Digbeth. Beyond the performers, in the centre of the newly pedestrianised Bridge, beyond the steps where people are sitting opposite the bottom of St Paul's Street, the Town Clock seemingly is guarding Bridge Street behind it. Bridge Street is undoubtedly the best street in the centre of Walsall with a lovely collection of Renaissance-styled Victorian retail premises.

*Above:* The Bridge in about 1930: as Corporation trams load up, Sister Dora looks benignly over the busy scene. In 1912 the poor lady's statue had been desecrated by being surrounded by the railings of the subterranean public toilets. The Corporation tram system had opened on 1 January 1904 with 28 tramcars operating five routes, all of which began at The Bridge. On the right is one wing of the George Hotel, a classically styled coaching inn built in 1781. It stood on the corner with Digbeth, which led into High Street, the latter being one of the oldest streets in Walsall and known as the site of the town's open-air market. The George Hotel was demolished in 1933. Overlooking the town, on the skyline, is St Matthew's Parish Church, an ancient structure which had been rebuilt in 1821 with a cladding of white Bath stone; this resulted in the church having a strange mixture of Georgian and Gothic-Perpendicular styles. *Birmingham Central Reference Library (Local Studies)*

The street had been redeveloped in the 1880s and it expressed the vibrancy and prosperity that had arrived in Walsall as it rapidly developed, after Sister Dora's 'finest hour', as a retail centre for the northern side of the Black Country. *D. R. Harvey*

*Below*: Within 50 yards of The Bridge in Bradford Street is the unusual 15-bay block of shops in a central arcade built in 1897 to the designs of Jonathan Ellis. The steel and cast-iron framing overlooking Bradford Street is delightfully exposed on the first-floor terrace, while through the somewhat unprepossessing centre entrance to the arcade are two malls with a glazed barrel roof. Above the entrance, in the top-floor assembly rooms, the arcade roof is marked by the elaborate gable end surmounting the pair of double pilasters. There is a distinct Art Nouveau feel about this block, where the four square bays on the second floor project uneasily over the almost Wild West look of the covered first-floor walkway. It is a lovely architectural gem! *D. R. Harvey*

# 2. Oak House, West Bromwich

Nestled into a corner site on Oak Road and Cambridge Street, just before the rows of Victorian terraced housing give way to inter-war council houses, is Oak House. This Tudor yeoman's house is a spectacular, largely timber-framed, gabled house. It was already well into its first 50 years when it was acquired by the Turton family, who had made a modest fortune out of their nail and forged blade-making industries based on their water-mills at Bromford and Greet, in West Bromwich. About the time of the family's acquisition of the house in 1634, a series of Dutch-gabled brick extensions were made at the rear of the property.

The drawing shows the southern aspect of the house from across the lawns. The brick extension on the left with the elaborate gables is for the morning room with, above it, a bedroom and the back staircase, while the smaller brick extension on the far corner is the dining room, which also has a bedroom above it. On the extreme right is the brick extension to the kitchen, also dating from the 1630s. Although these extensions occupy three sides of Oak House, they cannot be seen from the front. The interior of the house is also well preserved, with some good examples of furniture contemporary with the house as well as a 1,000-year-old oak chest.

*Top right:* That Oak House survives today is due to West Bromwich's well-known Victorian Alderman and sometime Mayor, Reuben Farley. The house changed hands twice during the 19th century, but its condition had deteriorated considerably, as can be seen in this photograph taken in about 1892, when the structure was all but derelict. It was Farley who, having realised the historical significance of Oak House, instigated the extensive restoration,

which took about three years. The house was purchased by Farley originally for his own use, but he presented it to the Corporation of West Bromwich on 29 October 1895, and it was first opened in 1898. After being used as a museum for half a century, it was transformed into a period museum with appropriate contemporary furniture in 1951. *Birmingham Central Reference Library (Local Studies)*

*Below*: The half-timbered frontage, with its attractive porch, perhaps still suffers from the late-Victorian restoration that saved the building for posterity. Almost certainly, the house was never black and white, but the wooden beams would have been their natural weathered oak colour of grey or light brown, which was not fashionable in the 1890s, but would probably be more historically accurate.

The photograph shows that the front still retains much of its original Elizabethan appearance, with a jettied first floor. This was done for many practical reasons, such as allowing rain to fall on to the ground away from the foundations, as guttering had not been invented! A more vital reason was that jettying made the house much more stable: as a test, put a large box on a tray on top of a smaller box and see how secure the whole structure becomes.

One unusual feature of Oak House is the Belvedere. This wooden lantern tower rises above the main gallery roof at chimney-top level and dates from the time of the brick extensions. It was referred to as a 'Lantern Tower' and was supposedly used by the Turton family as an observation tower during the Civil War when the Commonwealth-supporting family could get excellent views towards the Royalist stronghold in Dudley.
*D. R. Harvey*

# 3. Bull Ring, Sedgley

Anywhere called 'Bull Ring' usually refers to the medieval sport of bull-baiting. The market place would have market stalls and traders and frequently a pole or ring to tether a bull or even a bear; Staffordshire bull terrier dogs would then be set on the animal, and if it was killed the meat would either be given away to the poor of the parish or sold off cheaply. Present-day sensibilities make activities such as bull-baiting, bull-fighting and all field sports abhorrent to many, but when people were living lives that were nearer to the countryside than today, and when life and death were less sanitised, bull-baiting was a regular market-day entertainment, and frequently served a

useful purpose. The popularity of the Bull Ring name suggests that bull 'sports' took place throughout the Black Country; both the local Lower Gornal and Coseley have Bull Rings, while in Darlaston there is a 'Bull Stake'.

In the drawing, the tall three-storey building that dominated the corner of the Bull Ring and Dudley Street, Sedgley, from the late 1880s until its demolition in 1971 was occupied by the chemist, druggist and amateur photographer, J. T. Eggington. His shop was known as the Sedgley Drug Store, a term that perhaps seemed more suited to the 'Wild West' than part of the Black Country! Electric trams, operated by the Wolverhampton

District Company, replaced the steam tram 'shufflers' of 1886 on the hilly service between Dudley and Sedgley on 24 August 1901. At the time when this bogie tramcar rattled its way through the square, in about 1905, when the route had been extended to Fighting Cocks, the house behind it was occupied by the local doctor, conveniently located next door to the chemist. To the left of Eggington's shop, in Dudley Street, is the old stone wall that bounded the village 'pinfold', or pound, used to pasture animals before market day, while just beyond it was the village smithy.

To the right of the tram, in Gospel End Street, is the Old Court House Inn, whose fabric is a much older stone structure than the early 19th century façade suggests. It was the manorial court house, and cases were recorded here from 1535. Although it became an inn during the 1800s, the last court assizes were held there in 1925: 'The big judge, the little judge, the judges of assize!' (Thomas Hood). Standing behind the Old Court House is All Saints Parish Church; its tower is the only part of the medieval church to survive the 1829 rebuilding in local Gornal sandstone funded by the first Earl of Dudley at a cost of £10,784.

The open space in the foreground, from where the drawing was made, belongs to the Georgian Red Lion Inn. This was originally a coaching inn with facilities to change horses on the Wolverhampton-Dudley-Worcester stagecoach service.

*Below:* It was on 10 January 1886 that the Dudley, Sedgley & Wolverhampton Tramways Company opened its steam-powered tram service, which took only 40 minutes from terminus to terminus. Behind the pollarded trees in this mid-1880s picture is the Georgian house known as – though in reality it never was – the Manor House, which was demolished in 1968. The newly laid steam tram tracks, unusual for the West Midlands in being 'standard gauge' (4ft 8½in) are just visible in the road on the extreme right. In the centre and directly opposite the Red Lion is Hilton's House, which was still being used as a farmhouse. The crowds of children as well as numerous interested bystanders are watching a large 'dancing' muzzled brown bear. To present-day eyes this looks terribly cruel, but even in late-Victorian times this was an attraction rather than an unkind spectacle. *Birmingham Central Reference Library (Local Studies)*

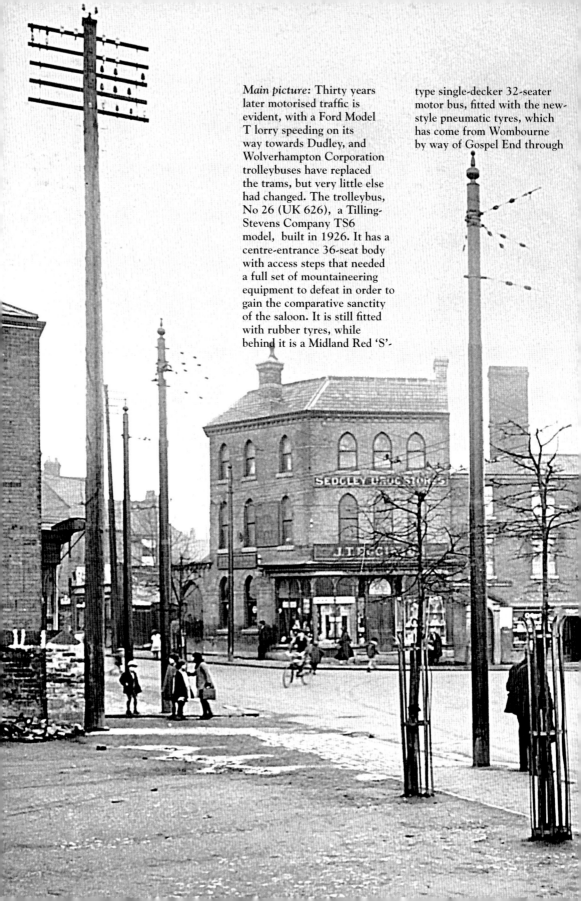

*Main picture*: Thirty years later motorised traffic is evident, with a Ford Model T lorry speeding on its way towards Dudley, and Wolverhampton Corporation trolleybuses have replaced the trams, but very little else had changed. The trolleybus, No 26 (UK 626), a Tilling-Stevens Company TS6 model, built in 1926. It has a centre-entrance 36-seat body with access steps that needed a full set of mountaineering equipment to defeat in order to gain the comparative sanctity of the saloon. It is still fitted with rubber tyres, while behind it is a Midland Red 'S'- type single-decker 32-seater motor bus, fitted with the new-style pneumatic tyres, which has come from Wombourne by way of Gospel End through the narrow entrance into the Bull Ring in front of the Court House public house. The doctor's surgery has now become a tobacconist and sweet shop, while next door is a grocer's shop owned by the splendidly named A. Spronson Vinrace.

*Below:* By 2004 All Saints Parish Church and the Court House public house have survived, as has the Red Lion Inn, but the cottages behind the single-deck trolleybus, which included Carni Fox's butcher's shop and slaughter house, were replaced by the Art Deco-styled Clifton Cinema in 1937. In 1998 the Clifton became a cinema-themed public house, after

languishing for many years as a bingo hall. The biggest change is that the two- and three-storey shops between Dudley Street and Dean Street, which were eventually all owned by Eggington's, were demolished in 1971 and replaced with a characterless block that does absolutely nothing for the Bull Ring area. *Bennett Clark Collection/D. R. Harvey*

*Above*: The present-day photograph of the statue is looking towards the south side of Queen Square, with the mock-Tudor frontage of the Woolwich Building Society and the varied buildings taken over by the Halifax behind the by now pedestrianised square. This was the site of High Hall, so today's buildings, saved for posterity, have a direct link to the times of the medieval markets in the centre of Wolverhampton. *D. R. Harvey*

*Right*: In the background of the drawing can be seen the Collegiate Church of St Peter. There has been a church on this site since Anglo-Saxon times and the present church, although rather spoilt by its rebuilding and over-zealous restoration, completed in 1865, still has an imposing presence in the city centre. The red sandstone nave dates from the mid-15th century, though the 14th-century tower was included in the Victorian rebuilding. In the foreground, set between Lichfield Street and St Peter's, is the Horsman Fountain. This is named after Philip Horsman, a local Victorian builder,

who surreptitiously paid for the designing and building of the Museum & Art Gallery in 1885. His covert philanthropy was eventually discovered and the fountain was built to commemorate his good deeds in the town. Alas, it is not known locally as the Horsman Fountain, but by the irreverent title 'the Big Squirter'! *D. R. Harvey*

# 5. Bratch Locks and Pumping Station

The Staffordshire & Worcestershire Canal was engineered by James Brindley at a cost of £100,000. It ran from the Georgian canal 'new town' of Stourport on the River Severn in a roughly northerly direction, skirting through the countryside to the west of the Black Country and passing the bottom of the 21 Wolverhampton Locks on the Birmingham Canal at Aldersley Junction. The next half-mile was the busiest on the Staffs & Worcs Canal, as it then passed Autherley Junction on the Shropshire Union Canal before heading to the northern end of the canal at Great Haywood on the Trent & Mersey Canal. This link allowed the china industries of the Potteries to get their wares not only to the Birmingham and the Black Country area, but also by way of the

River Severn on the shallow-draughted Severn trows down-river to Gloucester and the South West.

The Staffs & Worcs Canal was 46 miles long and had a total of 31 locks, including the rather lovely Brindley-designed Awbridge Bridge at Awbridge Lock, with its unusual circular weir, but the most famous and unusual is the picturesque set of locks at Bratch. The drawing shows the delightful octagonal toll office at the top of the flight of three interconnecting locks. At first sight 'The Bratch' looks like a staircase of three locks, but in fact it is a flight that James Brindley placed very close together after quickly rebuilding the locks in order to conserve water as the canal made the sudden descent across the Smestow Brook valley; this was done by rebuilding the original flight as three quite separate locks with the water pounds alongside. Today water can be seen jetting out from strange remote places into what appear to be these reed-lined side ponds.

The fall of the three locks is 30ft 2in, but the disadvantage of this unique flight is that it can only take one boat at a time going either up or down, which made 'The Bratch' a considerable bottleneck on the Staffs & Worcs Canal. Many a bargee paid the toll to use the locks, then 'paid the price' if they considered the locks anything other than three distinct locks.

pleasure craft as it has done since before the canals were nationalised in 1947, as the industrial traffic from the Potteries as well as from the links to the West Midlands had all but collapsed in the inter-war years. *D. R. Harvey*

*Bottom left inset:* The bottom of Bratch Locks is Bratch Waterworks, built in 1895 by Bilston UDC Waterworks to pump water from the 600-foot-deep boreholes in the underlying Bunter sandstone, with Bilston receiving its first water in 1896. It was designed by Baldwin Latham of Westminster and cost £6,133. The beautifully precise drawing shows off Mr Latham's extravagant structure to its best advantage, as the now preserved and listed building is now surrounded by trees (*left*), which in summer somewhat obscure it.

*Background:* The restored ramped towpath leads from the lowest lock up to the Georgian toll house from Bratch Bridge. Today the canal is used for

*Right inset:* The 1898 photograph shows the extravagantly Gothic-styled 'Xanadu', built in Ruabon red-brick with blue and beige brick decorations. It seems to have been inspired by the castles of the River Rhine rather than the cottages of the Smestow Valley! The two huge vertical triple-expansion steam engines installed in the new building were built by Thornewill & Warham of Burton-on-Trent, becoming operational in 1896. They were named 'Victoria' and 'Alexandra', and each was capable of raising about 1.2 million gallons of water per day. 'Victoria' was restored to operation in 1996, and is regularly used to demonstrate her impressive power, while her sister survives alongside. The large chimney was removed about the same time that the steam engines were replaced in 1960 by less romantic but more efficient gas turbine pumps,

but the decorative brickwork and the four tourelles, pointing skywards, have survived.
*Photos J. H. Hughes collection/D. R. Harvey*

# 6. The Stewponey and The Kinver Light Railway

The Stewponey & Foley Arms Hotel was a celebrated old coaching hotel on the Wolverhampton to Worcester Road, which today is the busy A449, and was only just over 2½ miles from the terminus at the Fish Inn at Coalbournbrook in Amblecote. The Stewponey stood opposite the Staffs & Worcester Canal, which was crossed by the Kinver Light Railway, originally on a wooden trestle bridge, at Lock 31. The Georgian building, shown in the drawing, was named after the Foley family, who had made their fortune by developing the iron forging industry in the River Stour Valley.

The other part of the inn's name was the rather unusual 'Stewponey'. Apparently an old soldier brought back to the West Midlands his Spanish bride from her home town of Estepona, in Western Andalusia in the south-west province of Malaga. They set up an inn on this site and named it after his wife's home town; needless to say, the original name soon became corrupted to 'Stewponey'. This original inn was nearer the corner of the Bridgnorth Road and the main Kidderminster Road than the 1930s pub that replaced it, and the drawing shows just how 'rural' was the location; even today the demarcation between the edge

of urban Stourbridge and the nearby countryside is sharply drawn.

The Kinver Light Railway opened on 4 April 1901 and the last recorded operation of this unusual 4-mile-long tramway seems to have been on Saturday 8 February 1930. It was built to the same 3ft 6in gauge as the rest of the tramways in the Black Country, which enabled it to link with the Dudley & Stourbridge line at the Fish Inn terminus at the junction of High Street and Enville Street. The reason for its construction was to take day-trippers to 'the Switzerland of the Midlands' at Kinver, some 5 miles away. The walks along Kinver Edge and the views over Shropshire were suddenly available to the nearby Black Country folk, and with the day-trippers, school parties and church outings came tea-rooms, ice-cream parlours and souvenir shops. In the Edwardian period the KLR was extremely popular, and on Whit Monday 1905 16,699 passengers were carried, with four trams running on a 20-minute headway. Parcels, post, fruit, vegetables and churns of milk were all

carried by the trams, and in winter freight traffic was frequently more remunerative than the carrying of passengers. The KLR brought not only day-trippers to Kinver but also new residents from the pre-First World War middle classes, so that by the time of the final closure a disputed date of 1 February 1930 the tramway had succeeded in transforming the village into a commuter settlement for nearby Stourbridge.

*Opposite below:* In the photograph taken in the early 1900s, the landlord, a Mr Elwell, is advertising that he is able to hire out cabs, motor cars and posting horses. On the left is bogie tramcar 51, on its way to Kinver. It has just descended Bridgnorth Road from Wollaston, running on the southern-side verge, and has reached one of the many tram track loops, this one outside the Stewponey Hotel. The tram, once the elderly lady has heaved herself into the central 'toastrack' section, will move off and immediately cross the main Wolverhampton to Kidderminster road before reaching the wooden bridge in the foreground. Tramcar 51 was one of three combination cars built by the Brush Company in Loughborough in 1901. These 56-seater single-deckers had an open section with cross-bench 'toastrack' seating in the centre of the body and small enclosed areas at either end. Because of their open sides, they were used only on the summer services.
*D. R. Harvey collection*

*Above:* In this drawing, looking to the left of the 1900s photograph, the top of the lock gate of the 10-foot-deep Stewponey Lock is visible and alongside the towpath is the restored octagonal toll office and the cottages alongside the once busy Stewponey Wharf. The taller section of the house was originally lived in by the lock-keeper, while the toll house today serves as an information centre and canal souvenir shop.

*Above:* Directly opposite the Stewponey Hotel there was a bridge that enabled the trams to cross the Staffordshire & Worcestershire Canal near the first lock immediately south of Stourton Junction, which linked the S&W to the heart of the Black Country by way of the Stourbridge Canal. One of the three large open 'toastrack' and combination trams of the Kinver Light Railway has just crossed the rebuilt canal bridge. Originally this bridge was a wooden construction, but the drawing depicts the later plate-girder structure that was similar to the replacement bridge built next to the Stewponey Lock on the Staffordshire & Worcester Canal. The Kinver Light Railway tram route crossed the River Stour before heading off across the private right of way to the Hyde and the terminus at Kinver.

*Bottom left:* The old pub was replaced to cater for the tram-riding tourists to Kinver, who had already been lost by the early 1920s, and the new building on the Kidderminster Road was a typically huge roadhouse-type pub that even boasted a lido, an open-air feature so characteristic of the 1930s, in the grounds at the rear. It catered for the pre-war motorists and coach parties on their way to or from the local countryside, but by this time probably not the nearby Kinver, which had by now largely lost the intensive tourist trade of the sunshine years of the Edwardian period. In later years, despite refurbishment, regular folk-singing nights and gaining a modern carvery, the Stewponey always seemed to be struggling for custom. The photograph was taken about two weeks after it had closed on 11 February 2002, showing it fenced off and awaiting demolition. In early 2005 the new luxury apartments and houses built on the site were being occupied, and the Stewponey and its adjacent light railway were just a memory. *D. R. Harvey*

# 7.
# *Galton Bridge, Smethwick*

Most of the earliest large structures made of iron and steel are well known, in particular the world's first iron bridge, which spanned the River Severn at Coalbrookdale and was built by Abraham Darby in 1779. This pioneering bridge gave its name to the Georgian riverside town of Ironbridge. Overseas, the 985-foot-high observation exhibition tower built by Gustave Eiffel between 1887 and 1889 is still a famous Parisian landmark. Yet in the Black Country, in Smethwick, is a real 'hidden gem', which briefly was the largest iron bridge in the world.

The original canal between Birmingham and Wolverhampton was opened in 1772, having been designed by James Brindley. By the end of the 18th century the canal had become a victim of its own success, being clogged with traffic, and, because it followed the contours of the land, locks were frequent. In 1790 the engineer John Smeaton took out three locks and lowered the summit of the canal by some 18 feet, between Brasshouse Lane and Spon Lane. Even so, with a summit at 473 feet, which was known as the 'Wolverhampton Level',

water was frequently in short supply. On 28 June 1824 Thomas Telford was called in by BCN management to try and solve the problems of water supply and congestion, and, on seeing the Brindley canal, referred to it as 'little better than a crooked ditch'. He took the dramatic view that the summit should be lowered to 453 feet (the 'Birmingham Level'), enabling the canal to take a straight line from Birmingham to Smethwick as well as taking out all the intervening locks. Telford's 'new line' was opened on 18 December 1829, and at its deepest point, where the depth of the cutting is 71 feet, he chose to build one of the great British bridges.

*Below:* Galton Bridge was named after Samuel Tertius Galton, a banker who served on the committee of the Birmingham Canal Navigation from 1815 to 1843. The bridge, seen in the drawing, looking westwards, doesn't just *cross* the canal, but vaults majestically over it. It has an arch span of 150 feet with a 26-foot-wide carriageway, and when it was built it was one of the largest iron bridges in the world. It was built by the Horseley Iron Works, which was also responsible for the construction of many of the iron bridges over the Black Country canals, including those at the top of the Delph Locks in Brierley Hill (qv).

The drawing, looking from the towpath, also shows the bridge of the old Handsworth Junction to Smethwick Junction line crossing the deep cutting of Telford's canal; this line was opened by the Great Western Railway on 1 April 1867 to link the GWR's main Birmingham to Wolverhampton line with the Stourbridge Railway's line. Although this important link was in operation for nearly 130 years, it suffered a lingering death from the time of the closure of the former GWR main line between Birmingham Snow Hill and Wolverhampton Low Level, and for years the railway tracks slowly gathered rust. The line was reduced to carrying a few freight trains a month, and it seemed that it would go the same way as many redundant and even some not-so-redundant railway lines. Yet in 1993 authorisation was given to West Midlands Passenger Transport Authority to re-open the link between Leamington Spa and Stourbridge. A new state-of-the-art high-level station was built above the existing Stour Valley line and over the Telford canal cutting at a cost of £4m, and was opened for normal service on Monday 25 September 1995. The lift towers of the new Galton Bridge station can be seen through the arch of the drawing of Galton Bridge.

If it were anywhere else, Galton Bridge would be highly regarded as one of the most significant pieces of British industrial archaeology! As it is, this Grade 1 listed structure is disgracefully hidden by the 1970s motorway link road, and although it was given a lick of paint in the early 1990s nothing else was done to restore the decking to its former glory, and it now serves only as a footbridge. It deserves better than this!

Today the bridge is well concealed by the ever-encroaching vegetation, but some idea of how this magnificent structure must have looked can be seen from this photograph, looking towards the then London & North Western Railway's Stour Valley railway line in about 1900. The relationship between the canal companies and the new railways was surprisingly cordial in the West Midlands, and this was one of the places where the railway company built its line alongside the canal. As a result of the opening of the railway, on 1 July 1852, an extra arch had to be built on the Smethwick side of Galton Bridge. *Commercial postcard*

*Below:* Galton Bridge is seen from the canal towpath looking in the other direction in October 2006. The 71-foot-height of the span looks even higher when viewed from below. The distant Galton Tunnel is little more than a concrete tube beneath Telford Way, and was only built in the early 1970s when the road, by now well hidden by the trees, was constructed. *D. R. Harvey*

# 8.
## *Windmill at Ruiton, Upper Gornal*

The high limestone ridge between Dudley and Sedgley overlooked the valleys of the River Tame to the east and the River Stour to the west. The western side of the ridge, always the more exposed, retained much of its rural nature until the second half of the 20th century, when a certain amount of urban expansion caused the farmland to retreat a little further to the west. Ruiton, a hamlet situated between Upper and Lower Gornal, was a windswept line of limestone-constructed cottages, workshops and mills that clung to the side of the western escarpment of the Sedgley-Northfield Ridge.

Although Ruiton was famous for its white sand, which was used as an abrasive throughout the Black Country, one of the

The drawing of the windmill shows it as it would have looked in the 1950s. It was in a derelict state by this time, having been last used in 1871, abandoned in the 1880s and left to crumble away. Not only had the farming largely disappeared from the nearby land, but so had much of the domestic nail-making industry. The inter-war years were for survival and not restoration, so the fate of old buildings like Ruiton windmill was not a priority. The sails of the mill are broken and only the masts of the sails remain as they stand drunkenly against the skyline.

main occupations of the 'locals' was to peddle rock salt around the Black Country for use as a food preservative. This salt was imported from the Droitwich area, as well as the Cheshire Plain, and the salt-sellers of Ruiton would stay away from home from Easter to the end of autumn. The name Ruiton is derived from an Old English word 'Ryge-tun', which means 'rye farm', though by the 18th century this had become Rewardine; the original name reflected the type of farming that took place on the exposed ridge and lower land to the west.

A reminder of this type of cereal farming and the exposed nature of Ruiton and the Gornals is found in the best preserved of the two windmills in the area. The windmill in Vale Street dates from the late 1820s and is made of the local limestone. In fact, it marks almost the south-eastern boundary of the use of the stone for building, and within about a mile Gornal limestone gives way to brick, even where the residential or industrial structure is more than 200 years old. There was a second Ruiton windmill, which was demolished in the 1950s. The locals always claimed that although the two windmills were on the top of the same ridge, there was never enough wind to turn both of them!

*Above:* The stone section of the mill has been restored, as have the houses that stand at right angles to Vale Street alongside it. This June 2005 photograph shows just how solidly built the old windmill is. It has windows set into the Gornal limestone at a higher level, while its entrance is in the garden of the old miller's cottages. What a conversation piece to have a windmill in your back garden!
*D. R. Harvey*

*Above:* The second photograph shows the double-width, somewhat long 18th-century stone cottage with the mill stump standing over it. The shape of the restored building, now divided into two cottages, suggests that when built it was the miller's house and the section immediately in front of the mill was his grain/flour barn where he probably kept his farm animals as well, all under the same roof as his own family. *D. R. Harvey*

# 9.
## Mushroom Green, Cradley

The hamlet of Mushroom Green lies to the north of Cradley Heath and to the north-east of Quarry Bank, and is within half a mile of the ultra-modern Merry Hill shopping centre. Yet in this quiet backwater is a 'hidden gem' that today is preserved as an outlying part of the Black Country Living Museum. Mushroom Green was a chain-making hamlet, with family firms such as the Kendricks, who were the last hand-made chain-makers in the settlement. Kendricks finally closed down in 1965 when the last owner, Harry Kendrick, died at the age of 80, leaving behind him a 'time capsule' that was to form the central attraction of the preservation area. Actually owned by Dudley MBC, the Mushroom Green chain-making shop and preservation area has been administered by the Black Country Society's Industrial Archaeology Group for the last 28 years, and once a week they employ a local hand chain-maker to demonstrate chain-making.

The drawing of the houses clustered around the green could have been made at almost any time, though the street light gives away its 2004 date. The houses are the successors to the original scattered squatter settlement, which, once established, developed quite quickly

in the early 19th century into the nail-making community known locally as 'Musham'. The local nail-makers were fiercely independent and this is reflected in the unplanned and haphazard way in which the houses do not align with each other. Presumably they found it difficult even to pass the time of day with each other, except in the local pub, which was ironically called 'The Cottage of Content'. The pub has long since gone,

but the building remains today as one of the hamlet's houses.

Mushroom Green is unique in that it captures a time around the end of the 19th century, albeit heavily sanitised, when the domestic chain-making industry was thriving. People lived out their lives producing chains by the thousand links at appalling piecework rates of pay. The large factories were in the Corngreaves area and were owned by

such illustrious chain-making companies as Samuel Woodhouse & Son and Henry Reece, while Richard Sykes, near Graingers Lane, was famous for its shackle pins. The most famous of all was Noah Hingley, who made cable chains for ships, but who had moved away to a better site in Netherton. Cradley Heath, Old Hill and Netherton became the chain-making centre of Britain, and as late as 1928, just before the Depression, 6,000 people were employed locally in the industry.

This photograph of the row of chain-makers' workshops in Cradley Heath in 1907 shows that much of the domestic industry was undertaken by women who worked in squalid conditions that cannot be imagined today! *Birmingham Central Reference Library (Local Studies)*

*Above:* Next door to one of the Mushroom Green cottages, originally painted white using locally produced lime, is one of the chain shops and its small brewhouse. The original domestic nail industry of the late 18th century had been displaced by machine-made nails in Harborne and other parts of Birmingham, so the industry that had grown up around the River Stour in Cradley Heath began to change to the making of chains. *D. R. Harvey*

*Below:* The Kendrick family chain shop after restoration in 1975; the family home next door had been demolished only a few years previously. *Birmingham Central Reference Library (Local Studies)*

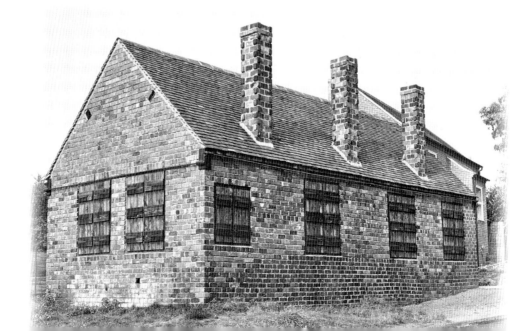

# 10.
## Harris & Pearson's brickworks, Brettell Lane, Brierley Hill

The Harris & Pearson Company was formed in 1852 when Peter Harris, who lived at The Elms on the corner of Bank Street and High Street, Brierley Hill, became a partner with George Pearson. They made firebricks from their works alongside the Dudley No 1 Canal and, as they needed to transport their bricks, they also became canal carriers. Harris & Pearson became the largest producer of the pure fireclay used for lining the retorts for the local Amblecote glass industry. Most coal seams rest on a layer of clay, which is usually grey in colour and contains the rootlets of the plants and trees from which the Carboniferous Middle Coal Measure seams themselves were formed. In the Brierley Hill area this was a rich seam of clay from which developed the extensive local brick industry. Additionally, in the Brierley Hill Trough was a layer of Etruria Marl, which was the basis of the famous Staffordshire Blue brick industry.

The company's head office was situated in Brettell Lane alongside the Great Western Railway station on the 'Old Worse and Worse' (Oxford,

Worcester & Wolverhampton) line. The drawing shows off the gaunt symmetry of the office-cum-gatehouse building, constructed in 1888 in a variety of blue and yellow bricks, the former being the famous Staffordshire Blue bricks that were found as kerbing along virtually every canal towpath in the country. It was built not only as the company headquarters, but also to show off the quality and variety of the company's products. Harris & Pearson was taken over by E. J. & J. Pearson in 1931; these were local coal and iron masters who had premises and mines in the Delph and Amblecote areas, but were restrained from the type of growth they wanted by the local Stourbridge Firebrick Association. During the inter-war period the company expanded by also taking over four other brick-making companies.

After a ten-year campaign to save the building, which had become derelict after it was vacated in 1990, the offices benefited from a £869,000 restoration back to their original

condition, completed in January 2005 by William Sapcote & Sons Ltd, who also refurbished the interior. The owner, West Midlands Historic Buildings Trust, has just announced the sale of the Grade II listed building for a six-figure sum as offices for a business consultancy firm.

On the Brierley Hill side of the offices the Old Crown public house still survives, but the old Kings Arms inn has long since been demolished, while opposite is the New Wellington, which had been the brewery tap for the famous and much missed Simpkiss Brewery. Local pubs had their own brewhouse that supplied the iron, brick and glass furnace workers with beer, and all the local ale houses had 'pot boys' to supply the sweating workers.

*Below:* **The old head offices standing on Brettell Lane, seen here before restoration, are the sole reminder of when the extraction of fireclay and its manufacture into fireclay bricks to line the thousands of Black Country industrial furnaces was the main industry around Silver End, Brierley Hill and the Delph.** *D. R. Harvey*

*Above:* The same building in 2006 after restoration work had been completed.

*Right:* Clay extraction was still taking place in 1967 in the area to the south of the Stourbridge Canal on the other side of Brettell Lane in Withymoor. Gradually, however, all the local fireclay and brickworks closed down, and among the last was the Clattershall Works, owned by Harris & Pearson. It is seen here in November 1974, when the brickworks had been recently closed and the firing kilns were awaiting demolition. In the centre is one of the rectangular furnace chimneys; amazingly a number of these furnaces with their distinctive chimneys survive today, and one is seen in January 2005 with a working narrowboat tied up near to the Seven Dwellings Bridge. *Both D. R. Harvey*

The 3ft 6in-gauge electric tram service along Brettell Lane was introduced on 26 July 1899 using small 28-seater single-deck tramcars supplied by the Brush Electrical Engineering Company in an orange and grey-white livery. Beyond Silver End and Harris & Pearson's, Brettell Lane dropped around 150 feet towards the junction with High Street, Amblecote. The open-top double-deck tramcar seen here in Brettell Lane is one of the 22 ERTCW four-wheelers that entered service in 1901. Seen when almost new, it is standing between the Vale Street passing loop, just behind the photographer, and the Park Street loop, almost at the bottom of the hill. At this time Brettell Lane was lined with continuous rows of late-18th-and-19th-century cottages, such as those on the left, and a mixture of terraces and tall three-storey houses

on the right. The Dudley & Stourbridge tramway closed on 1 March 1930, having succumbed to competition from Midland Red motor buses.

Today all these buildings have gone, except for a few late-Victorian premises now used as shops at the bottom of the hill, which would have been virtually new when the young lads wearing the knickerbockers were standing just behind the horse and cart. The remaining buildings have been replaced, and today Brettell Lane is a bland road lined with trees and car showrooms, while facing it across the junction with the main Stourbridge to Kingswinford main road was the short lived Crystal Glass Centre, which after a barely ten year life was closed and converted in to shop units including a 'Tesco Express' and a 'Halfords'. *Commercial postcard*

# 11.
# Dudley: the Castle, the Market Place and the Fountain

During the Civil War Dudley Castle was a Royalist garrison, but it did not suffer the same fate of destruction as many other castles in the country, when it was captured by the Parliamentarians of Oliver Cromwell in 1646. After the Civil War it survived as the home of the Earl of Dudley, whose illegitimate son, one Dud Dudley, began his unsuccessful quest to exploit the local resources of coal in the early 1660s in nearby Tipton, and thus set up a train of events that altered the landscape and economy of the area for ever. The need to use another source of fuel for the iron industry became necessary because of the almost complete depletion of local timber supplies used for making charcoal. At this time there were already almost 20,000 smithies in the area, and nail-making was already well established, so there was rapid change from a small market town into a centre of industry in the Black Country.

Dudley was given its Market Charter some time in the early 13th century, and even before the Industrial Revolution it had a thriving daily market, which survives and thrives to the present day as an important market centre for the area straddling the watershed on which it stands.

Dudley grew up as a settlement beneath the Saxon castle, built on one of the three geological inliers of limestone that are located in the area. The castle is perched on the top of the hill, with its 14th-century ruined keep visible from the town centre and, even more impressively, from the River Tame Valley to the east. The drawing shows Dudley Castle on the top of Castle Hill, looking down on the famous Dudley Zoo, which opened on 5 May 1937, and the rest of the town centre. The view is from the Market Place, and also shows on the right St Edmund's Church in Castle Street, with its attractively proportioned tower. Known locally as 'Bottom Church', this Georgian church was built in brick and stone, replacing a medieval building, and was consecrated in 1724.

*Below:* At the far end of Dudley's Market Place is the ornamental fountain. This was built on the site of the old Town Hall and next to Middle Row, a row of buildings down the centre of High Street. The Old Town Hall had been built in 1653 by Thomas Caddick and was a heavily mullioned brick-built structure that seemed to have the same function as a medieval moot hall. Latterly it was used as a magistrates' court, a police station and a gaol. The demolition of the properties in Middle Row took place between 1835 and 1851, while the Old Town Hall was swept away in about 1860.

The fountain is a real gem of mid-Victorian philanthropy, being a gift to the town by the 11th Earl of Dudley in 1867 to encourage temperance; however, this was something of a false hope, as alongside it was the Dudley Arms Hotel and opposite was Lester's Board Inn, one of the few old buildings to survive to the present day. In the drawing is one of the large gas lamps that surrounded the fountain; these were removed in about 1899. The fountain is surmounted by two busts of horses apparently lying beneath the finial female figure (perhaps the ultimate Black Country wench!), and was built of Portland Stone in an Italian Renaissance style. Designed by James Forsyth, before being placed in the Market Place the statue was exhibited at the 1867 Paris Exhibition.

*Right:* On 26 July 1899, the same year as the four ornate street lamps were removed, the Dudley & Stourbridge Company began to operate its tram cars between the two towns by way of Brierley Hill. One of the original single-deck trams, with seats for just 28 people, moves out of the Market Place towards the junction with Stone Street. Facing the tram's somewhat exposed driver is the climb up High Street towards St Thomas's 'Top Church'. It is therefore unusual to find a postcard view of Dudley with the ornate gas lights, which apparently guarded the fountain, and the electric tramcars together, as this situation could have only lasted for literally months. *D. R. Harvey collection*

*Below:* The interior of the motte of Dudley Castle in 1870: the buildings inside the castle wall were the 16th-century domestic accommodation constructed when Dudley Castle had all but ceased to be a defensive bastion. The ruins seen in this amazing Victorian photograph were the result of a terrible fire

on 24 July 1750. It is said that some illegal counterfeit-coin-makers caused a fire in one of the cellars and the subsequent conflagration burned for three days. *Birmingham Central Reference Library (Local Studies)*

*Below right:* The 18-foot-high fountain, which became dry and neglected for many years, survived only by the skin of its teeth, having first been threatened with removal as long ago as 1924. Over the intervening years this piece of high Victoriana was allowed to deteriorate and it was only

after the Market Place was pedestrianised in 1983 that the fountain was restored, though unfortunately it is only used as a focal point, such as the preparations for the 2004 Remembrance Sunday parade and ceremonies. *D. R. Harvey*

*Top right:* This photograph of the Market Place was taken in about 1946, and some of the street lights still have wartime blackout shades. Looking in the opposite direction from

the drawing, it shows the canvas covers over the two rows of market stalls. As ever, the stall-holders are doing a good trade with their fresh fruit and vegetables in those days of food rationing. Their customers have to compete with what little traffic there was at the time – noticeably there are fairly few private cars. In the background there are two pre-war Midland Red buses manufactured locally by the company at its Carlyle Road Works in Edgbaston. The double-decker is a front-entrance 56-seat SOS FEDD, while the single-decker on the extreme right is a GHA-registered SOS SON dating from 1940. *Birmingham Central Reference Library (Local Studies)*

## 12.
## *St Luke's Church, Blakenhall*

throw out the rule book! As a starting point, Robinson used a sandy yellow brick coupled with black in a series of horizontal bands around the church at various levels, as well as picking out the pediments over the doors and windows. Even the clerestory windows, which look like three circles, are in fact within a border of decorative brick-surrounded spherical roundels.

In the nave the pillars are thin, doubled piers, but even here the quirky architect put them longitudinally rather than transversely. The tower is on the south-west of the nave and has a spire, but even here the apparently simple task of designing a spire on top of a tower was not straightforward. The result makes it look as if Mr Robinson had several attempts at totally different designs, then, because he couldn't make up his mind which was best, simply combined all of them to produce something as fanciful, yet successfully soaring skywards, as this! The detailed drawing looking from Sunbeam Street, opposite the Sunbeam Motor Factory complex, reveals particularly well just what a strange combination of styles Mr Robinson employed in his design.

Upper Villiers Street was best known as the location of the Sunbeam Motor Works. It also has on the corner of Moor Street undoubtedly one of the 'hidden gems' of the Black Country. For sheer effrontery and joie de vivre, St Luke's Church takes some beating – it is a wonderful piece of Victorian architectural rhubarb! This red-brick church was completed in 1861 and is in itself nothing of any great architectural moment. Yet the architect, a G. T. Robinson of Leamington, just went completely overboard when it came to the spire and the detailed decoration. At a time when the Victorian's Gothic styling was beginning to look solid and staid, this church's appearance began to

*Above:* Located to the west of Dudley Road in the Blakenhall area of Wolverhampton, St Luke's Church is slightly off today's main routeways into the city centre. In the 1920s and 1930s it was surrounded by Victorian terraces and, latterly, blocks of multi-storey flats and maisonettes, which at the time of writing were being prepared for demolition. Across on the other side of Upper Villiers Street was the huge Sunbeam Works, from which the last car left in the mid-1930s after the company was taken over by the Rootes Brothers. The huge site, with many of its buildings dating back to before the First World War, remains largely untouched since then, although the large individual factory blocks have been sub-divided to provide small individual units. Upper Villiers Street was perhaps a more important road into the centre of Wolverhampton than it is today, but the decline of the area has left St Luke's Church somewhat beached in a sea of waste-ground awaiting redevelopment.

The first photograph *(previous page)* shows the west end and tower of the church, while the second *(below)*, taken from the south-east in Moor Street, confirms how the tower is all but detached from the tall nave, while on both sides of the nave are low-roofed aisles.
*D. R. Harvey*

## 13.
## *The Two Spires and the Market Place, Wednesbury*

Wednesbury can trace its origin back to Anglo-Saxon times and the top of the hill was first recorded as a religious site dedicated to St Bartholomew in 1210. Gradually, through the medieval period, the town changed from an agricultural-based settlement into a market town, with a Market Charter granted in Queen Anne's reign in 1709. When the road between Wednesbury and Bilston became a turnpike in 1766, the town was placed on the stagecoach road between London and Shrewsbury, which of course brought more prosperity.

But Wednesbury was also sitting on huge reserves of coal, and after the opening of James Brindley's Wednesbury Canal on 6 November 1769, when the first coal from the Wednesbury area arrived in Birmingham its cost was halved overnight and the expansion of the South Staffordshire coalfield was assured, supplying the insatiable appetite of the furnaces and factories of its larger neighbour.

Standing on the top of Church Hill overlooking the town is the Parish Church of St Bartholomew and next to it is the Roman Catholic Church of St Mary. Their location is hardly hidden, but despite their prominent position on the skyline, both churches seem to be taken for granted. The drawing shows the two buildings on top of Church Hill, set among the small houses that clustered around them, with the Georgian Old Library House next to the southern main entrance. The area around the two churches could almost be a village on its own. Although the Woden Inn is the only Victorian remnant at the town end of Church Street, a few pre-Victorian houses survive in Church Hill. Until the early 1950s, in Ethelfleda Terrace – named after King Alfred's daughter, who was supposed to have fortified the hill in around AD 916 – there was a row of three-storey Georgian terraced housing, while in Hall End and parts of Clark and Wellcroft

Streets Victorian rows of houses nestle below St Mary's in much the same way as they did when the church was still quite new.

St Bartholomew's, with its attractively shaped spire and clock faces set into the tower, is the taller of the two. This soot-blackened church looks as though it dates from about the early 13th century, but it is a much later structure, with the nave and north transept dating from 1827, while the east end and the south transept were completed in 1890 to the designs of Basil Champneys. The Roman Catholic Church of St Mary of 1874 is built in a lovely mellow red brick with black brick mullions and decorations, and was designed by Gilbert Blount. It has a thin copper steeple atop an open bell tower, though the steeply pitched roof of the nave looks rather too large. The need for a Roman Catholic Church in Wednesbury became necessary because in the town and surrounding areas there were more than 3,000 itinerant

Irish labourers who lived lives of extreme poverty and hardship. An Irish priest, Father George Montgomery, who had been born in Dublin in 1818 as a member of a Protestant family whose patriarch was a sometime Lord Mayor of that city, came to Wednesbury in 1850. He had converted to Catholicism and trained for the priesthood at Oscott College, completing his training in 1849. Seeing the plight of the Irish workers, he virtually financed St Mary's Church and the associated church hall himself.

Individually, the two churches are architecturally quite ordinary, but together they compliment each other as well as dominating the hilltop above Wednesbury.

*Below:* This view of St Bartholomew's Church in Church Hill shows it off to its best effect, while the copper spire of St Mary's peeks over the brow of the hill.
*D. R. Harvey*

*Above:* In the years immediately before the First World War, when the Market Place was newly dominated by the George V Coronation Clock, unveiled in November 1911, and when young girls wore smocks, every male over 16 wore a cap or hat, and the weather always seemed to be sunny, Walsall Corporation tramcar 10, a vestibuled car built in 1903, comes through the Market Place from the terminus at the bottom of Lower High Street at St John's Church. *Birmingham Central Reference Library (Local Studies)*

*Below:* Fortunately many of the older buildings have survived, so that today the Market Place is a rather splendid conservation area, as can be seen in the photograph taken on 27 April 2005. The old street market stalls have gone, but the central area is still an open space and the majority of the shops in and around the Market Place and High Street belong to local retailers rather than chains. It is so refreshing to find a town centre that hasn't been redeveloped to look just like everywhere else! *D. R. Harvey*

The Wednesbury Branch was the first section of the Birmingham Canal Navigations to be opened and as a result brought prosperity to the town, changing it irrevocably from a small market town into one of the main extraction and industrial areas of the Black Country.

In the centre of Wednesbury is the Market Place, nowadays separated from the two churches by Bullen, the 1970s road built to bypass the town. The wedge-shaped Market Place was characterised by the Georgian and Victorian buildings such as the Old Golden Cross Inn. This area is an oasis of Victoriana, which has survived nearly

intact either by accident, or latterly by design, although the loss in 1965 of the George & Dragon Hotel was a great pity.

*Above:* This photograph of the bustling Market Place dates from about 1890 and shows the market stalls, all equipped with canvas shelters, attracting shoppers and bargain hunters in a time when the daily market was regarded as more important than the permanent retailers located around the perimeter. South Staffordshire Tramways Company steam tram No 26, built by Beyer Peacock of Gorton in 1884, hauling a Falcon-built double-decker trailer car, shuffles through the pedestrians as it passes on its way to Walsall. *Smethwick Library*

# 14.
# Netherton Tunnel portals at Tividale and Darby End

Netherton Tunnel cuts through the Sedgley-Northfield Ridge between Oakham and close to the 866 feet of Turners Hill. This ridge separates the two halves of the Black Country, with the Stour Valley lying to the south and the Tame Valley to the north of this, the main English watershed. The ridge is a very complex structure, being made up of Silurian limestones in the north, Carboniferous Upper Coal Measures and, around Turner's Hill and Rowley Hill, a large intrusion of dolerite or, as it is known locally, 'Rowley Rag', which, although looking very hard, exfoliates badly (weathers like an onion) and is only suitable for road stone.

Running beneath this ridge is the famous 3,027-yard-long Netherton Tunnel, and the first drawing shows the western portal and the canalside cottages just beneath the Tividale Aqueduct. These cottages date from about 1830

and have survived almost certainly because of their location, which is difficult to reach other than by foot or barge. The aqueduct carries James Brindley's old Main Line over the straight Netherton Tunnel Branch from the nearby Dudley Port Junction, almost a mile away on the New Main Line, which had been surveyed and designed by Thomas Telford in the 1820s. The canal tunnel was opened in 1858 to relieve pressure on the nearby Dudley Tunnel. It went into the record books as the eighth longest canal tunnel in Britain, though closures over many years brought its position up to second after Blisworth Tunnel on the Grand Union Canal.

When it was built, Netherton Tunnel was sufficiently wide to accommodate within it towpaths on both sides of the waterway; it was also wide enough for narrow boats to pass comfortably inside. Unlike in the older 3,172-yard-long Dudley Tunnel of 1792, where the only way through was 'legging', the towpaths on the new canal enabled horses to pull their charges through. The additional aid of gas lighting, installed at the time of construction, made the whole experience much less arduous. By 2007 some of the brickwork in the tunnel was in a poor

state and the towpath had been closed. Repairs will hopefully take place soon.

*Above:* **Walking across Turners Hill above Netherton Tunnel there are a number of strange-looking, round brick-built structures. These are the tops of the ventilation shafts for the canal, which can be easily identified when on a narrow boat travelling through the tunnel as places where water drips down your neck!**
**D. R. Harvey**

At this southern end of the tunnel there are some overnight moorings, which originally formed a canal basin serving the long-since-closed Warrens Hall Colliery No 1 pit. This basin is on an embankment that stands above the Dry Dock public house, whose bar is made up of the hull of a barge, while alongside the canal is an excellent information centre and tea-room. Looking from the visitors' centre, the blue brick entrance to the southern end of the Netherton Tunnel is just visible beyond the Netherton Roving Canal Bridge, while the famous Cobb's Engine House stands beyond the Windmill End Bridge in the foreground and the partially hidden Swan Pool. *D. R. Harvey*

*Right inset:* At the other end of Netherton Tunnel is Darby End, today a grassy area that has a timeless and peaceful feeling in a once intensely industrial site. Cobb's Engine House, the gaunt remains of which are seen in the second drawing standing above the tunnel's southern portal, is officially known as Windmill End Pumping Station, and was built in 1831 by Sir Horace St Paul to house a stationary beam steam engine. This was used to pump water out of the coal mines beneath the area, which were riddled with geological faults causing water to pond up and pour into the mines. It must have been a pretty large engine as it was regularly pumping 1.6 million litres, or nearly 352,000 gallons of water, per day out of the mines and into the adjacent canal.

The narrowboat emerging from the Tipton end of Netherton Tunnel is on its way to Birmingham, having come through the tunnel from the south near Cobb's Engine House at Bumble Hole. Following the Netherton Tunnel Branch, it will pass the towpath cottages seen in the first drawing after passing beneath Brindley's 'crooked ditch' before turning right at Dudley Port Junction. *D. R. Harvey*

# 15.
## *Bantock House, Bradmore, Wolverhampton*

The 43-acre Bantock Park stands in the triangle of land formed by Bradmore Road, Finchfield Road and Broad Lane in the Bradmore area of Wolverhampton to the west of the city centre. Located at the eastern side of the park is the delightful Bantock House, which, from the road, is well concealed by the rows of mature trees around the perimeter.

Bantock House was originally built as Merridale Farm and dates from about 1734. The Classically styled frontage seen in the drawing is at least 70 years newer than the rear, and has a pleasantly pillared porch and regular-shaped Georgian windows. Merridale Farm House was purchased by local industrialist Thomas Bantock in 1867 and it was subsequently renamed Bantock House.

It was Thomas Bantock's eldest son, Albert Baldwin Bantock, who began a large refurbishment of the house in the last years of the 19th century using interiors inspired by William Morris's Arts & Crafts Movement. The interior of the house has Delft tiled fireplaces, a wood-panelled main entrance hall and ground-floor rooms, and extravagant plaster-moulded ceilings. It has a large collection of locally manufactured japanned ware, steel jewellery and enamelware, which largely dates from the Edwardian period. Quite often such rather dark though artistic interiors were destroyed as tastes changed, but as Albert Bantock grew older he resisted the need to modernise the interior. He became an Alderman in the town and was Mayor of Wolverhampton on three occasions, in 1905-6, 1906-7 and 1914-15.

After his death in 1937 the house was bequeathed to the Corporation, though it was not opened to the public as a museum until 22 April 1948, having been used throughout the Second World War as a requisitioned military establishment. As a museum it displays locally manufactured products, even including a Clyno 9hp saloon of the late 1920s and various motorcycles which were made in Wolverhampton such as AJS and Sunbeam.

*Above & below* The front and rear of Bantock House. The rear is part of the old farmhouse and has a much less planned look to it than the elegant frontage. Also at the rear is the Dutch Garden, alongside the Victorian conservatory; it is a lovely quiet place to sit and admire the well-maintained flower beds in this walled suntrap. *Both D. R. Harvey*

# 16.
# *Moseley Old Hall, Featherstone*

Standing between the Wolverhampton boundary and the M54 motorway is the delightful and historic Moseley Old Hall. To reach the house today, a dead-end lane has to be negotiated, and from the outside it looks like any ordinary 19th-century brick-built country house. Yet beneath the red brickwork of the house lies an Elizabethan timber-framed building with a splendid main staircase dating from about 1600 as well as numerous priest's holes, which would eventually find use in the most unlikely of circumstances.

The Old Hall was built by Henry Pitt of Bushbury on land bought from the Codsall family. His daughter, Alice Pitt, married Thomas Whitgreave, whose family were Roman Catholics, and the

house subsequently had several priest's holes for concealing clerics and their religious items. Although Catholics, the Whitgreave family were Royalists and it is during the English Civil War that the house had its moment of fame.

Five days after his Royalist Army had been defeated at the Battle of Worcester, in the early hours of 8 September 1651, Prince Charles arrived at Moseley Old Hall disguised as a woodcutter. He was on the run from the Cromwellian Army and for the first time since the battle, in what was then called the Priest's Room, he was able to sleep in a bed. On 10 September the Parliamentary soldiers arrived at the house, but fortunately they were spotted coming down the narrow lane and this gave the future King time to hide in the priest's hole located behind a trap door in the bedroom. The space was about 4 feet high, and it was many hours after Cromwell's men had gone that Prince Charles was able to emerge from his life-saving hiding place. Under cover of darkness, Charles made his escape the following evening and made his way by a circuitous route to Shoreham on the South Coast, then into his nine years of continental exile, before returning in 1660 to claim the throne as Charles II. In the house is displayed Charles II's letter of thanks to the family who helped to conceal him during the four days he was on the run after the Battle of Worcester.

After this dramatic period Moseley Old Hall returned to its former role as an ordinary Elizabethan-built country house, though its subsequent Victorian encasement in brick undoubtedly enabled it to survive; what is most surprising, however, is that its interiors were left largely unaltered, so that today visitors see very much of what the fleeing Prince would have seen in 1651. The front and side of this doubly 'hidden gem' are shown in the drawing, demonstrating the splendidly unplanned frontage as well as the more symmetrical four-gabled southern elevation.

The Whitgreave family received a pension after the Restoration, and they finally sold the Old Hall in 1925; after several more years being used as a farmhouse, it was bought in 1940 by a Mr Wiggin of Bloxwich. He was a member of the family that owned the Old Hall Stainless Steel Company, and after undertaking a lot of remedial work they passed the house to the National Trust.

*Thanks are due to David Lewis, the Estate Manager, who allowed me access to the Hall before opening hours.*

**Above:** The somewhat unprepossessing main entrance of Moseley Old Hall leads to the wonderful 17th-century interior.

**Right:** On the ground floor on this south side of the Hall was the lady's sewing room, which overlooked the 17th-century-styled knot garden with its beds of lavender and herbs of the sort used in the house at the time as the Civil War. Among the flowerbeds and the lawns are banks of primroses, a few of which were originally planted about ten years ago; they gradually spread and mixed with a wild clump of cowslips. Both have been cross-fertilised to form the very rare yellow oxlips seen in this 2006 photograph of the knot garden and loggia.
**D. R. Harvey**

# 17.
# *Wolverhampton Low Level railway station*

The early history of Wolverhampton Low Level station is rather complex. A station using standard gauge (4ft 8½in) tracks was opened nearby by the Shrewsbury & Birmingham Railway on 12 November 1849. Legal disagreements between the S&B and the London & North Western Railway, and the use of the Stour Valley line into Birmingham New Street station, allowed the initiative for new lines to be switched to the Oxford, Worcester & Wolverhampton Railway, also known as the 'Old Worse and Worse', which reached its new Low Level station in Wolverhampton on 1 July 1854. Having opened its 'broad gauge' (7ft 0¼in) line between Banbury and Birmingham, the Birmingham & Oxford Junction Railway, owned by the Great Western Railway since August 1848, was opened to Wolverhampton Low Level on 14 November 1854.

The drawing shows the old Low Level station area in its until recent semi-derelict state, albeit mothballed since becoming a listed building in 1986. On the right are the high blue-brick retaining walls above which are the catenaries for the electrified train service into what was the old High Level station. Various proposals have been made to restore the building, including making it into a Wolverhampton Transport Heritage Museum. The main station buildings are in the middle of the drawing, while the remnants of the platforms are on the left. It was here for more than 15 years that a marooned parcels van stood with ever-more faded blue paint on a tiny section of weed-intruded rails. If Birmingham Moor Street station can be restored to its former Edwardian glory, then surely this gem's restoration is of prime importance. In 2006 work started on an extensive redevelopment of the old station building which includes shops offices and places of entertainment.

The Great Western Railway's broad gauge line from Birmingham Snow Hill station went through West Bromwich, Wednesbury and Priestfield Junction before reaching Wolverhampton. Broad gauge tracks were also laid beyond the station to Stafford Road engine shed and as far as Oxley Sidings. This was as far north as Brunel's broad gauge was allowed to go, as the Regulation of Gauge Act, passed on 18 August 1846, prevented any

further expansion of the wider baulk-laid tracks. The last broad gauge trains ran between Birmingham Snow Hill and Wolverhampton Low Level on 31 October 1868.

Wolverhampton Low Level station's two-storey booking hall was built in a very plain, almost Classical style in Staffordshire Blue bricks. Unfortunately, the station became increasingly shabby in the period following the 1948 Nationalisation, with unpainted woodwork and a scruffiness with which

even the most ardent former employee of the Great Western Railway could not cope. Then, when the electrification of the old LNWR line between Euston, Birmingham, Wolverhampton High Level, Stafford, Crewe and the West Coast Main Line was completed in 1967, the old station was doomed. The result was that services to Birkenhead Woodside from Paddington were withdrawn, and after Sunday 5 March 1967 both Wolverhampton Low Level and Birmingham Snow Hill ceased to be main-line railway stations. The local services, which still comprised 24 stopping trains per day in each direction, were using diesel multiple units, but despite the lines' projected closure being rejected by Barbara Castle, the Minister of Transport, British Rail disgracefully adopted the policy of making the service unpopular by reducing the frequency and size of the trains. After 4 March 1968 the service from Wolverhampton Low Level was reduced to just three trains each way per day, while all the stations on the increasingly derelict former main line became unstaffed halts after 3 May 1969.

This photograph can be dated by the presence of the two parked GWR buses at the far end of the Low Level station forecourt or carriage yard. This bus service to Bridgnorth by way of Compton Road began on 7 November 1904 with three single-decker Clarkson steam buses, but these had problems climbing Hermitage Hill on the way out of the River Severn's steep-sided valley, and were replaced in January 1905 by 20hp Milnes Daimlers. Two of these petrol-powered buses are parked in front of their new corrugated iron garages in the distance, which dates this picture to about the year of their introduction. They are the only motorised vehicles on the station forecourt, while parked outside the Booking Office are a couple of Hansom cabs and a four-wheeled carriage. *D. R. Harvey collection*

Inevitably, financial losses grew as passengers were encouraged to go elsewhere, so the Low Level station was closed to passengers after the 17.47 service left on Saturday 4 March 1972. The station buildings had become a Parcels Concentration Depot on 6 April 1970, but even this closed on 23 October 1985, having lost its rail connection four years earlier.

*Left*: Dating from the last year of King Edward VII's reign, this photograph shows the enormous overall roof of the Low Level station. Weighing more than 400 tons, the roof was 575 feet long and had a span of 115 feet. Standing at the mouth of this cavernous stygian gloom with the four platforms disappearing into the blackness are two GWR locomotives, one designed for express passenger work and the other for local stopping trains. On the right is the larger express locomotive of the 'Bulldog' Class. Built with curved frames, locomotive No 3310, named *St Just*, was a 4-4-0 built as part of William Dean's 'Duke' Class in February 1897. It was enlarged with a bigger boiler in September 1908, and it looks as if this photograph was taken not long after its conversion into the more powerful 'Bulldog' Class. Simmering away on the left is small 0-4-2T No 550, built at the nearby Stafford Road Works as long ago as 1869 and used for lightly loaded branch-line passenger trains. The overall roof was subsequently discovered to be unsafe due to corrosion, and was taken down during a process that took several months from 2 October 1933, after which the station continued to be used throughout the Second World War and into the post-1948 Nationalisation period. *G. M. Perkins collection, courtesy of R. S. Carpenter*

*Above*: The computer generated image of the redeveloped station site.

For most of the period between the last quarter of the 18th century and the middle of the 20th, the Pensnett area of Kingswinford was littered with collieries and gin pits while canal arms and, later, the GWR's Kingswinford branch meandered their industrious way taking coal away and serving the numerous local iron foundries. Just out of Kingswinford village on the climb up High Street towards the area of brickworks located to the north of High Oak, Pensnett, is a little haven that even today looks like a village green snuggling around a pretty little church, but less than 100 years ago must have looked totally out of place in this terrible industrial landscape.

*Bottom left*: The basic fabric of the station is still intact today, even having one set of rails, but the poor old dear is desperately crying out for some 'tender loving care'! It is one of the few reminders of the Great Western Railway's presence in the Black Country. *D. R. Harvey*

# 18.
# *St Mary's Church, Kingswinford*

Parts of St Mary's Church, Kingswinford, date from the 12th century, and this delightful building, with its massive squat tower, was the parish church of the huge Kingswinford parish, which until 1831 included Wall Heath, Wordsley and Brierley Hill. Much of the fabric of the building is Victorian and dates from the 1843 rebuilding, but there are traces of Georgian stonework as well as evidence of a much older building.

For example, in the space between the lintel of the vestry doorway and the arch over it, known as the tympanum (*see drawing opposite*), there is an outstanding decorated Norman stone carving depicting a large winged St Michael slaying a large dragon.

In the churchyard there is a very old stone pillar, which appears to be the shaft of a medieval preaching cross, as well as a

tombstone with grooves made by passing Royalist troops who were sharpening their swords in the late summer of 1651 before going on their way to fight and be defeated at the Battle of Worcester. The old church was later the burial site of many of the local industrial families such as the Corbyns, Hodgetts, Scotts and Bendys.

The foundation stone of Holy Trinity Church at Wordsley was laid on 27 August 1829, it was consecrated on 9 December 1831, and for the next 15 years the new Wordsley church was the parish church of Kingswinford; the parish records were transferred there and St Mary's was reduced to a chapel-of-

ease. However, the effects of mining and industrialisation began to dramatically increase levels of urbanisation and population size, the large parish rapidly became unwieldy, and was broken up in 1846. A much smaller Kingswinford parish was created, giving St Mary's back its former status in 1848, having been closed due to mining subsidence from 1831 until its restoration was completed two years earlier.

The drawing, looking from the main road, shows St Mary's Church from the village green, together with the elaborate lych-gate, where pall-bearers rested before carrying a coffin into the church. To the right is the War Memorial to the fallen of the two World Wars.

Opposite the village green alongside High Street, Kingswinford, is the Old Court House. This dates from the late 18th century and matches the surviving court house in the Bull Ring at Sedgley and the long lost one in Dudley. While it was built as a hostelry, Lord Ward used all three premises as his local manorial court houses, a function later taken over by the town magistrates. The court houses' main function was to act as the equivalent of the pre-enclosure village strip lynchet courts, in that they enabled the local landowner to oversee and regulate the allocation and use of his lands by his tenants. Today, like its 'twin' in Sedgley, the Old Court House in Kingswinford is a public house and restaurant. *D. R. Harvey*

The original 18th-century cottages on the north side of the green are shown in this photograph dating from the late 1890s, which also shows the original lych-gate. The July 2004 view provides a closer view of the entrance to the churchyard and also shows the original medieval stonework in the tower, which ends around the base of the clock. *D. R. Harvey collection/D. R. Harvey*

The village green is a triangular grassed and tree-lined area leading off the High Street and is frequently used to park bridal wedding cars. It is sufficiently large that in July 1996 preserved Crossley DD42/6 double-decker No 2489 (JOJ 489), owned by one of the authors, was used as the wedding vehicle, though the low foliage prevented the bus from getting really close to the churchyard entrance. *D. R. Harvey*

# 19.
# *Lightwoods House, Bearwood*

Standing in the grounds of Lightwoods Park on the border of Bearwood and Birmingham is Lightwoods House. It was built in 1791 for a Leicestershire maltster named Jonathon Grundy, who named his new house after the nearby Lights Wood. The house is constructed of brick but has had stone dressings and stucco decorations added in the 19th century. The Grundys and the related Willetts remained in the house until 1865, when it was sold for £8,700 to George Caleb Adkins, a local Smethwick-based soap and red lead manufacturer, but after the death of his son in 1902 it appeared

*Right:* **A survival in the park is the Edwardian bandstand with its delicate wrought-iron work, seen on the snowy Boxing Day of 1968.**
*B. W. Ware*

that the house and its grounds would be sold off to property developers who were interested in continuing the rapid wedge-shaped growth of urbanisation across Atkins Lane that had taken place in the 1880s and 1890s.

The house and park stood between this development and, across the park to the boundary with Birmingham, the then named Beech Lane, later to become Hagley Road West. Fortunately, although the house and grounds were put up for sale, A. M. Chance, a member of the Chance glass-making family of Spon Lane, purchased the estate for £13,000 and donated it to Birmingham Corporation. This intensely political move effectively blocked the southern housing expansion of Bearwood to the Beech Lane boundary. Birmingham immediately turned the gardens into a public park with a large ornamental pool between the house and the main road.

Lightwoods House itself, shown in the drawing from the western end of the park, has been used variously as a library and tea-rooms, as well as a stained-glass artist's studio in more recent years. At one time, on this Bearwood site, there was the secluded Shakespeare Garden in which grew all the flowers and plants mentioned in the Bard's plays. What a shame it did not survive!

*Below:* **An Edwardian postcard of Lightwoods House with children standing next to the ornamental pool and 'the ladies' taking their ease by sitting on the bench.** *Commercial postcard*

*Above*: This photograph of Hagley Road West, Bearwood, was taken on Wednesday 18 June 1930. It shows a four-year-old Midland Red SOS FS-type bus, HA 3544, standing at the edge of Lightwoods Park, which can be glimpsed through the boundary trees. This shows just how close Lightwoods House and its park was to the boundary with Birmingham, as the sign in the foreground reveals. *Birmingham Central Reference Library (Local Studies)*

# 20.
# *Sedgley Beacon, Sedgley*

The drawing of the famous Sedgley Beacon shows a strange stone signal tower, 50 feet high and 7 feet in diameter, ignored and unloved, and in a desperate state of repair. Yet the tower is a symbol of Sedgley, and commands an affection that is surprisingly strong, as it can be seen from all over the area. The Sedgley-Northfield Ridge constitutes part of the main watershed in England, with the land to the west being drained by the River Stour system leading into the Severn Valley, while the land to the east drains into the River Tame whose waters eventually reach the North Sea by way of the River Trent. The highest point of this Silurian limestone ridge is Sedgley Beacon, with a height of 777 feet, and while the top of the hill was left largely undisturbed by the industrial growth of the 18th and 19th centuries, several quarries excavated limestone for use as a furnace flux, while the nearby Beacon Hill quarry had an on-site lime kiln to produce lime as fertiliser and white lime wash, used to paint cottages and farm buildings.

*Left:* Known locally as 'the big whistle', Sedgley Beacon can still be seen from the surrounding lowland, though these days it has to compete with a number of radio and telecommunications masts, which rather detracts from this strange folly's attractiveness. Today it is in dire need of restoration; the internal spiral steps are partially worn away or even missing, which, combined with the general decay of the stonework and mortar, means that an estimated £150,000 needs to be spent on the structure. *D. R. Harvey*

The top of the hill at Sedgley therefore provides an excellent vantage point, and as a result it has been used since medieval times as the location of a signal beacon as part of a chain of either warning or celebratory fires across the West Midlands. There was a permanent tower on the site in the 17th century, but this was replaced in 1846 when Lord Wrottesley, a well-known local astronomer, built the present stone structure for use as an observatory, while the lookouts were added later by a Mr Petit, a local landowner. In Queen Victoria's Golden Jubilee year of 1887 a beacon was lit in a brazier at the top of the tower, and over the succeeding century this has been repeated to celebrate other Royal anniversaries.

While the view back towards Sedgley is rather uninspiring, the view to the north, as the Silurian limestone ridge gently dips away, reveals an area of open grassland. However, beneath the green sward lies a sunken reservoir built by the South Staffordshire Water Company between 1962 and 1972 just prior to the formation of the Severn-Trent Water Authority in 1974. This underwater reservoir, which replaced an earlier one built in 1893 and is connected to the Shavers End reservoir in Highland Road, Dudley, has a capacity of 45 million gallons, supplying Coseley and Sedgley with water from the Hampton Loade intake site on the River Severn. The land has been successfully landscaped and no one would know that it was there, as can be seen in the photograph over the sloping heath and grasslands looking towards Wolverhampton. *D. R. Harvey*

# 21.
# *The Greyhound public house, Bilston*

High Street, Bilston, has one of the really forgotten 'hidden gems' of the Black Country. Although Bilston has the rather splendid Regency buildings in Mount Pleasant, towards the western end of the town in High Street, the buildings are generally much more mundane. The street itself has been much altered since Wolverhampton Corporation's 25 trolleybus route stopped running along it on 27 October 1964 and has been truncated at either end, enabling most of Church Street to become pedestrianised.

At the western end of High Street is a wonderful half-timbered reminder of the sort of buildings that were found scattered across medieval South Staffordshire 200 years before it became the Black Country. Known today as The Greyhound & Punchbowl, this genuinely old public house was known for many years as The Greyhound. It was built as Stowheath Manor House in 1457, though several different dates in the 1450s are quoted.

It replaced a much earlier moated building in Chillington Lane, nearer to Wolverhampton, with the original house being located between the Bilston and Willenhall Roads. The Manor of Stowheath was quite large as it included Bilston, Willenhall and the eastern side of Wolverhampton. Originally this delightful old building had eight gables, signifying that it was once a lot larger and more important; today only five remain, suggesting that a certain amount of demolition took place in the early 19th century.

*Below:* Perhaps surprisingly for a building of this age, there is only one section that has any jettying, by which the successive upper storeys overhang the lower floors. This created a very stable structure and enabled the upper floors to have more floor space than those at ground level. The jettying can be seen below the left-hand gable which stands slightly back from High Street. This majestic building still retains its Jacobean plaster ceiling despite having been a pub since 1820. By the early 20th century the old place was in a very dilapidated state but was restored under the auspices of J. A. Swan in 1936. This black and white postcard dates from

the 1960s, when the old Savoy picture house was still open, and shows the building in its restored state. *Commercial postcard*

*Above:* Today, although adorned with a somewhat gaudy sign, the Greyhound & Punchbowl public house is a delightful survivor from a time when Bilston was a small agricultural village in the days before the Industrial Revolution. *D. R. Harvey*

# 22.
# Delph Locks,
# Brierley Hill

The Stourbridge Canal was authorised by an Act of Parliament in 1776 and linked the Staffordshire & Worcester Canal at Stourton with the Dudley No 1 Canal. This enabled goods manufactured in the Black Country to be exported by way of the canal system and the River Severn to the port of Gloucester. The Stourbridge Canal was built on the principles of James Brindley in that it attempted to follow the natural contours of the area. As a result it meanders across the countryside until it reaches its junction with the Dudley No 1 Canal near 'The Black Delph', so called because of the large number of collieries in the area.

The exploitation of the nearby blue fireclay deposits at the Leys would be accelerated by companies such as the predecessors of Harris & Pearson of Brettell Lane (qv) as they now had the canal on their doorstep. In addition, just beyond the top of the Delph Locks was the giant Round Oak steelworks, which initially used the canal as a means of supply and export, but it was still being used until the mid-1960s to take away clinker and other waste. The steelworks helped to maintain the Dudley No 1 Canal's prosperity long after canals

*Above:* **The remnants of the long-abandoned ninth lock can be seen in the drawing, with overgrown vegetation almost hiding the derelict lock gates and the surviving brickwork.**

elsewhere were little more than drainage ditches. After the closure of Round Oak Steelworks in 1982, only two years after the steel works receiving an industrial award for its outstanding production record over the previous three years, the canal fell into even greater disuse, although the local Dudley Council did help the funding of the renovation of the Delph Locks.

The Dudley No 1 Canal had to descend from its 441-foot contour level at Brierley Hill down to the 356-foot level of the Stourbridge Canal system. In order to achieve this, the Delph Locks were constructed, and opened in 1779.

As seen in the drawing, they form one of
the most dramatic flights of locks in the
West Midlands, and it is not just because
of the number of locks that the Nine
Delph Locks are so well-known. That
number can easily be beaten elsewhere
in the West Midlands – the Birmingham
Canal Navigations main line from
Aldersley Junction into the centre of
Wolverhampton has the famous 'Twenty-
One' with a rise of 132 feet in about 2
miles, while the 'Stourbridge Sixteen'
takes the Stourbridge Canal up a rise of
148 feet in little over a mile between
Wordsley Junction and Brockmoor. But
it is the spectacular nature of the Delph
Locks that makes them such a 'gem', as
they fall 85 feet in barely 500 yards.

Construction of the locks began in
July 1777 and each of the original nine
had a fall of 10 feet. However, financial
difficulties meant that the flight was not
opened until the second half of 1779, and
initial fears about a lack of water were

overcome by the construction of the Fens Pools reservoir on 'Pensnett Chase'. The problem was that the locks became too popular as a link between the BCN system and the river port at Stourport. With freight tonnage increasing by 50% to 95,000 tons in 1824, traffic congestion and a shortage of water caused the link to stagnate, even though the newly

introduced railways were beginning to have an adverse effect on freight traffic anyway. The result was that as late as 1857 work began on realigning the nine Delph Locks to the west and introducing a straight flight of locks rather than the original curved flight. The original top and bottom locks were retained, but the six intermediate locks all date from this rebuilding.

*Opposite and below:* There were originally nine locks, and in the middle distance next to the inter-war council houses in this 1950s photograph can be seen the old lock-keeper's cottage. Both the drawing and the photograph show the view from Mill Street Bridge in Brierley Hill, and in both can be seen the 1858 roving bridge built by the Horseley Iron Works in Tipton. This spans the entrance to

the original line of the Nine Locks, with water getting into the first old pound, and carried the horses over to the eastern side of the flight so that they could pull the narrow-boats without interruption. The long building on the left of the flight was the old stables, which are used today as maintenance workshops for the locks. *Birmingham Central Reference Library (Local Studies)*

Today the Nine Delph Locks, still called nine even though for 150 years there have only been eight, is recognised as one of the most photogenic flights of locks in Britain and has taken on a new lease of life with the increase in the use of pleasure craft and 'touring' narrow boats.

*Left*: The 1970 photograph was taken alongside the first of the new locks and shows the old brick-kiln chimneys at the Leys, while the spoil heaps from the old open-cast clay workings can be seen in the distance.

*Bottom left:* The present-day photograph was taken some 35 years later on 14 January 2005. In the intervening years the locks have been renovated and the distant open-cast mining and the nearly all the brickworks have been lost. On the site of the former, where for 150 years blue clay was extracted to be fired up in the kilns at the Leys to produce the famous Staffordshire Blue bricks, is the large Withymoor housing estate. *Both D. R. Harvey*

*Below:* The view from the bottom of the Delph locks near to where the Dudley No 1 Canal becomes the Stourbridge Canal at Delph Road shows the water overflowing down the side weirs. This occurs only when the flight of locks is full and water cascades down the overflow weirs. When the flight was rebuilt, this would have been the nearest thing to a natural waterfall that the locals were ever likely to see! *D. R. Harvey*

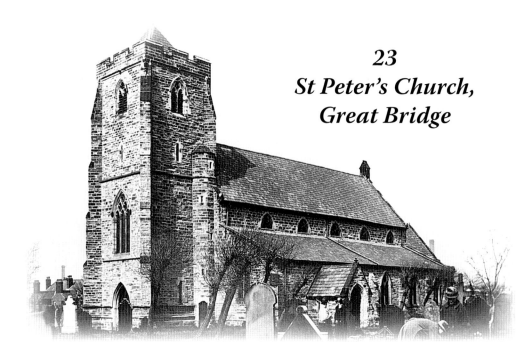

# 23
# St Peter's Church, Great Bridge

Hidden away in the tree-lined churchyard in Whitehall Road is St Peter's Church, Great Bridge. This attractive Victorian church was built in the Decorated Gothic Revival style using Gornal sandstone, and by keeping the embellishments simple the result was a church that could easily be mistaken for a genuine 14th-century building. The architect, a T. Johnson of Lichfield, designed it with a wide nave and arcades of octagonal piers capped with flat Decorated arches. St Peter's was consecrated by the Rt Reverend John Longsdale, Bishop of Lichfield, on 28 June 1858, having cost around £4,000 during its year of construction. It was built on land owned by William Johnson and Sir Horace St Paul, and survived almost undisturbed until it was

**Left:** Although partially masked by the abundant foliage, the west window can just be seen in this photograph of the west door and north aisle. *D. R. Harvey*

*Above:* The drawing, showing the view from the south-east, just in front of the church hall, shows the building to its best advantage.

*Opposite top:* St Peter's Church in seen in about 1925, looking from the south-west towards Whitehall Road. One really good thing about this church is that the architect paid a good deal of attention to the detail, so that for instance the individual size of the stonework making up the fabric of the church actually looks as if it is 14th century. The south porch leads into the narrow southern aisle, while the nave, with five disappointingly small clerestory windows on each side, rises towards a quite steeply pitched roof. The nicely proportioned west tower has a tall narrow window with reticulated tracery that consists of circles drawn at the top of the window to create a net-like appearance. *Terry Price collection*

nearly destroyed in a fire in November 1966. Fortunately, only five months earlier, a new church hall had been opened and blessed by the Venerable Basil Stratton, Archdeacon of Stafford, and this hall was used for services for

more than a year until the restoration of the church was completed.

In 1898, on vacant land adjacent to the church, an extravagant vicarage was built by the then incumbent vicar, one Henry Jesson, who paid for most of the work himself. It was a huge house with two extended wings at either end of the frontage, an Arts & Crafts open brick porch entrance and rooms in the dormer attic. Unfortunately it was demolished in 1980 and replaced by housing association flats.

Despite its 1967 replacement roof, St Peter's has a timeless, almost village-like quality about it, as seen in the drawing of the church and its churchyard. At first sight it looks far older than it actually is, and, together with the large grassed churchyard, provides a tranquil haven in the heart of Great Bridge.

At the eastern end of the nave is a much larger altar window with three trace columns as opposed to the two in the west end of the tower. This window can be seen behind the 1864 tombstone dedicated to the 19-year-old daughter of George and Sarah Crowther.
*D. R. Harvey*

# 24.
## *Soho House,*
## *Hockley, Birmingham*

Although strictly speaking not in the present-day Black Country, Soho House in Soho Avenue, Hockley, has links with the birth of the Industrial Revolution in the West Midlands. It was the home of Matthew Boulton (1728-1809), and for a time this elegant house was the centre of philosophical thought, scientific investigation and industrial creativity and initiative in late-18th-century England, and thus one of the country's most important meeting places. It was here that the Lunar Society met on nights with a full moon, turning Soho House from a home into 'an inn for the entertainment of strangers'. As well as Matthew Boulton, William Murdock, who successfully developed gas lighting, and James Watt, who perfected the stationary industrial steam engine, were members of the Lunar Society. Other Society luminaries included Joseph Priestley, a vicar who, as well as being against the Established Church, also discovered oxygen. There was Erasmus Darwin of Lichfield, the grandfather of Charles Darwin, who was a renowned physician, botanist, inventor, researcher into cloud formation, evolutionary theorist as well as a poet. Other members include William Herschel, the astronomer who discovered the planet Uranus, Josiah Wedgwood, the potter and tableware manufacturer, and John Smeaton, a leading Georgian organist who also designed steam engines as well as the first Eddystone lighthouse. These were seriously influential people whose ideas and discussions were considered to be dangerous by many of their peers, but as dedicated capitalists they wanted to improve the quality of life for the very people who feared them!

Standing at the top of Hockley Hill at around 450 feet above sea level, Soho House overlooks the valley of Hockley Brook in Soho, just over the then Handsworth boundary in Smethwick, where Boulton had built the famous Soho Manufactory (qv). The lovely detailed drawing of the front of the house shows the house as it looks

*Below:* **Before the house became a girls' boarding school in the 1890s, Thomas Lewis, a well-known Birmingham-based Victorian photographer, took this picture of the front of Soho House and its ornamental gardens, and it is in this condition that the house appears today. Behind it is St Michael's Church, Soho Hill, built in 1855 in a Decorative Gothic style to the designs of W. Bourne, although the very visible spire was not added until 1868.** *Birmingham Central Reference Library*

today, having been lovingly restored as a museum owned by Birmingham City Council. It is a wonderful 'time capsule', showing a period, more than 200 years ago, when this Georgian house was owned and lived in by one of the most influential men in British industrial history.

Soho House was the home of Matthew Boulton from 1766 until his death in 1809. He had acquired the lease on the house on Handsworth Heath in 1761, building work having only begun four years earlier. Boulton employed Samuel Wyatt, a local architect, to make the house habitable and, during the construction of the new reception rooms, Boulton designed and had installed a central heating system. In 1796 James Wyatt, Samuel's son, designed virtually a new house, adding a third storey. The new frontage was built with seven bays, and included a semi-circular Ionic porch.

*Right:* The porch was restored to its original state in 1957. It has two classically styled Ionic-capitalled pillars and is flanked by two of the four Ionic pilasters that extend to the entablature of the house. *D. R. Harvey*

*Below:* In true classical Georgian style, the ground-floor and first-floor windows are the same height, while those in the second floor are half-sized. This gives the full height of the building a very aesthetically balanced appearance at the front, though the rear aspect, shown here, is extremely plain in comparison, while remnants of the original two-storey house are visible on the right. *D. R. Harvey*

The drawing shows the remaining terrace of 18th-century workman's cottages in Foundry Row, which have survived as the sole reminder of the Soho Manufactory. That they avoided demolition is most surprising, as the end block nearest the present post-war Avery gatehouse was demolished to make way for the new entrance. These cottages represent a well-hidden Black Country 'gem', and are historically important as, on his return to Soho from Cornwall in 1799, William Murdock lived in one of them. Heater moved into Sycamore Hill House, just west of the nearby Queen's Head Road and close to the main Soho Road in Handsworth.

# 25.
# Soho Manufactory and the Avery Scales factory

Matthew Boulton began building his Soho Manufactory in 1761 on the site of one of the many mills constructed on and using the water power from Hockley Brook, which crossed the present-day Factory Road near Soho Pool. Here the river formed the boundary between Handsworth, Aston and Birmingham and the valley was quite wide, enabling the manufactory to expand into this large open space. The vast Soho Manufactory produced such a wide range of goods and machinery that almost certainly the legend of Birmingham being the 'town of one thousand and one trades' was coined here – and, yes, Soho manufactured coins! It began by manufacturing buttons and buckles, but began to fabricate boxes, trinkets and jewellery

using silver and gold as well as cast iron. Gradually this enterprise began to expand into making japanned wares, silver-plated steel, ormolu clocks and candelabra, as well as a wide range of weaponry.

The list of products would itself fill a volume, but it was Boulton's association with James Watt, which began in 1774, that made the Soho Manufactory's name. Watt brought the latest stationary steam engine developments to the Soho Manufactory and his steam-powered pressurised pumping engines revolutionised industrial growth in this country. These engines were not only

This is one of about four photographs taken in 1851 when the Soho Manufactory was still structurally sound, but vacant. The sheer size of the building is quite startling, equalling the size of some of the Victorian cotton mills of Lancashire being built at about the same time that Soho was closing down. There were four such blocks as this, arranged in squares with workshops and warehouses employing more than 1,000 men. The picture shows the front aspect of the Soho Manufactory to be a rather plain three-storey building with a central four-storey entrance, the latter boasting a pair of classically formed Ionic-capitalled pillars and a tower-like structure surmounted by a cupola. It was, rather like I. K. Brunel's Great Eastern steamship, a leviathan before its time, so that once the management driving forces died, the impetus to keep this multi-faceted manufacturing centre turning out its wide range of products disappeared. The photograph itself is quite fascinating, as the print was taken from a Platinotype wet collodion glass plate negative, and is one of the earliest photographs of a specific building ever taken in the West Midlands. *Birmingham Central Reference Library (Local Studies)*

sent around the country to pump water out of mines, but additionally provided power to run vast numbers of lathes, capstans, weaving looms and manufacturing equipment in mills and factories across Britain. William Murdock's experiments with gas lighting, which began as early as 1792, enabled the Soho works to be lit to celebrate the Peace of Amiens in 1802 between England, France, Spain and Holland. The pioneering work undertaken by Boulton, Watt and Murdock at Soho enabled the new industries to become mass-producers

and heralded in 'consumerism' before the term was even invented! The death of James Watt the younger in 1848, who had lived in the beautiful Jacobean Aston Hall, spelled the end of the Soho Manufactory, and it was closed down soon afterwards. The assets were sold off, leaving the buildings to stand empty for more than a decade before being razed to the ground and disappearing without trace under some scattered late-Victorian tunnel-back housing and a variety of heavy industrial premises.

Just to the north of the Birmingham Canal was the 25-acre site of the Soho Foundry Works, built by James Watt in 1796 to supply the components for his steam engines. The foundry was taken over in 1895 by W. & T. Avery to expand their manufacturing of scales and weighing machines, at the behest of William E. Hipkins, the new Managing Director, who was one of the 120 First Class passengers to go down on the RMS Titanic when it sank at 2.20am on 15 April 1912 with the loss of 1,523 lives.

**Below left:** In this late-19th-century photograph of Avery's occupation of the site, the horse and cart traffic is the only form of transport in Foundry Row, which has become the main road through the factory behind the imposing cast-iron gates and the equally imposing bowler-hatted gatekeeper! The buildings on the left are the 1890s offices. *Birmingham Central Reference Library (Local Studies)*

**Below right:** The Soho Foundry name survives on this imposing gateway on Foundry Lane, which frames the excellently restored row of cottages, opposite the Black Patch recreation park. *D. R. Harvey*

*Below:* In the mid-1890s a pioneering South Staffordshire Tramways electric tramcar, No 42, carrying a good load of passengers, stands outside the somewhat shabby Old Court House. In those days of the horse and cart, pedestrians milled about the road with little regard for the traffic – or lack of it! This tiny tram is one of the 1892 Brown Marshall 40-seaters that had two 15hp motors and is in the earliest reddish-brown livery. It is working on the Darlaston to Mellish Road service, which, together with the Wednesbury to Bloxwich route, was the second overhead trolley system to operate in Britain. *Commercial postcard*

*Opposite top* Next to the Court House is the Council House. This was opened on 27 September 1905, having been designed by James S. Gibson in 1902; he was the winner of a nationwide competition for the proposed building. When the foundation stone was laid on 29 May 1902 by HRH Prince Christian of Schleswig-Holstein, Queen Victoria's son-in-law, it was Walsall's first Royal visit for 250 years.

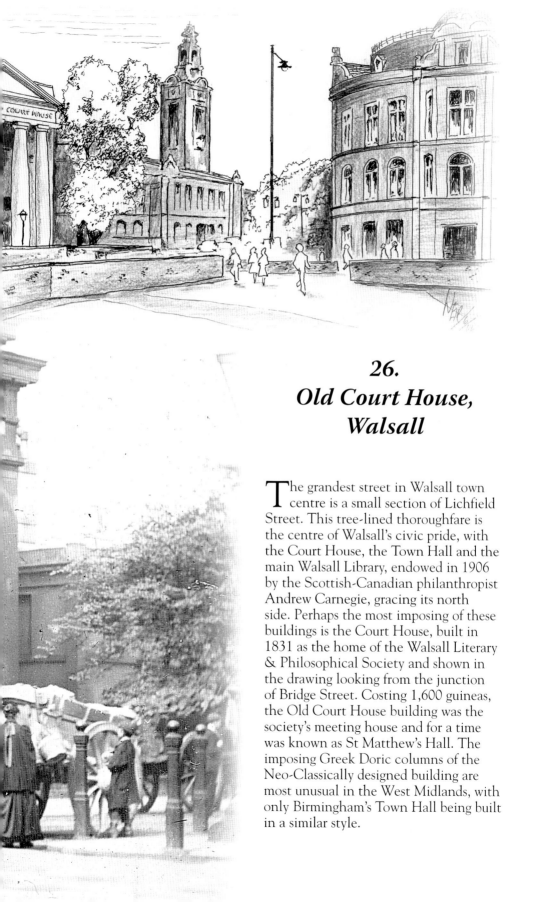

# 26.
# *Old Court House, Walsall*

The grandest street in Walsall town centre is a small section of Lichfield Street. This tree-lined thoroughfare is the centre of Walsall's civic pride, with the Court House, the Town Hall and the main Walsall Library, endowed in 1906 by the Scottish-Canadian philanthropist Andrew Carnegie, gracing its north side. Perhaps the most imposing of these buildings is the Court House, built in 1831 as the home of the Walsall Literary & Philosophical Society and shown in the drawing looking from the junction of Bridge Street. Costing 1,600 guineas, the Old Court House building was the society's meeting house and for a time was known as St Matthew's Hall. The imposing Greek Doric columns of the Neo-Classically designed building are most unusual in the West Midlands, with only Birmingham's Town Hall being built in a similar style.

The Council House is a wonderful piece of Edwardian Baroque architecture with a symmetrical frontage, an offset tower and a large number of decorative sculptures by Henry Fehr, who was a regular exhibitor at the Royal Academy. The exterior Hollington sandstone from Staffordshire is as crisp today as it was when it was first cut, and as a result the Fehr sculptures and low-relief frieze of local manufacturing look as good as new. During its lifetime the Court House has had a varied career, being Walsall's County Court for most of the 20th century and in recent years a rather imposing restaurant and public house owned by Wizard Inns.

**Right:** By about 1935 the Court House and the Town Hall can be seen in much better condition, as an unidentified AEC 'Regent' bus approaches one of the new Belisha beacons in Bridge Street; these were named after the then Minister of Transport, Mr Leslie Hore-Belisha. Opposite the Court House is Windridge's pram shop, located in another Baroque-styled Victorian building.

*D. R. Harvey collection*

**Below:** On 29 January 1999 a Travel West Midlands Volvo B6LE, No 563 (P563 MDA), works into Walsall town centre on the 370A route and passes the impressive Town Hall and the newly restored Old Court House public house, which are the two architectural 'gems' of Walsall's Lichfield Street. *D. R. Harvey*

## 27.
# *Farley Clock Tower, Carter's Green, West Bromwich*

The Farley Clock Tower at Carter's Green was built in 1897 to commemorate Reuben Farley (1826-1899), five times Mayor of West Bromwich and the first Freeman of the municipality because of his philanthropic work in the expanding Victorian town. The clock tower was designed in a Gothic Renaissance style by Edward Pincher and includes decorative panels, one of which is a picture of Farley himself, another being Oak House, which he purchased and renovated for the benefit of the town, and another showing West Bromwich's Town Hall.

The clock tower is square and made of brick, and above the four clock faces is an openwork cupola that sits somewhat disappointingly on the top.

The drawing of the Farley Clock Tower shows it as it would have looked in the Edwardian period with the long-since-demolished terraced cottages in Dudley Street disappearing towards the nearby Great Western Railway main line between Wolverhampton and Birmingham. The Methodist Chapel, with its Decorated-style windows, would have been in its heyday at this time, and had yet to suffer the many years of dereliction before being pulled down in 1970.

For many years at the junction of Dudley Street leading to Great Bridge and Dudley, and Old Meeting Street going towards Hill Top and Wednesbury, was the Methodist Chapel, opened on 8 May 1876 on the site of a former hostelry called the Old Junction Inn. The Methodist Chapel was closed in about 1949 and demolished in 1970 to make way for the West Bromwich Expressway.

Two South Staffordshire bogie tramcars wait at the shelter alongside the Farley Clock Tower in about 1920, with one of the commemorative plaques, bearing the bust of Reuben Farley, clearly visible. This view of Carter's Green has hardly changed over the years with many of the properties on the left hand side of the High Street surviving to this day, as seen opposite. *Commercial postcard*

*Above:* Looking back towards Great Bridge, the open fretwork of the cupola on the top of the clock tower is allowing light to pass through it. Behind the clock is the Methodist Chapel, and to the right of the South Staffordshire tramcar are the aforementioned retail properties that date back to the early years of the 19th century. The date of the photograph is around 1902 as the tramcar, No 15, a 60-seat bogie car built by Brush of Loughborough, looks still quite new. The tram is going to Dudley on the service from The Woodman Inn at the Handsworth boundary next to the Hawthorns football ground, which commenced operation on 30 May 1903. *A. Wilson, Travel Lens Photographic*

*Below:* The photograph taken in January 2006 is looking towards Carter's Green and beyond to West Bromwich. Carter's Green has managed to retain many of its early-19th-century buildings, and the Farley Clock Tower is in extremely good order: the four-faced clock is working, keeps the correct time and is beautifully lit up at night. The low reliefs around the base of the clock have survived and visible from this angle is the head of Reuben Farley, the philanthropic Alderman of late-Victorian West Bromwich. It does seem a shame, however, that the Alderman is facing away from the town that he served so well. *D. R. Harvey*

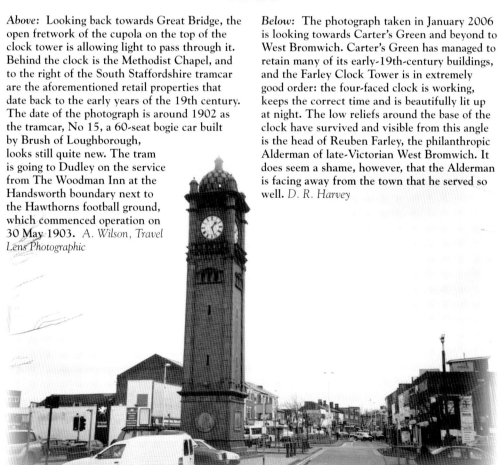

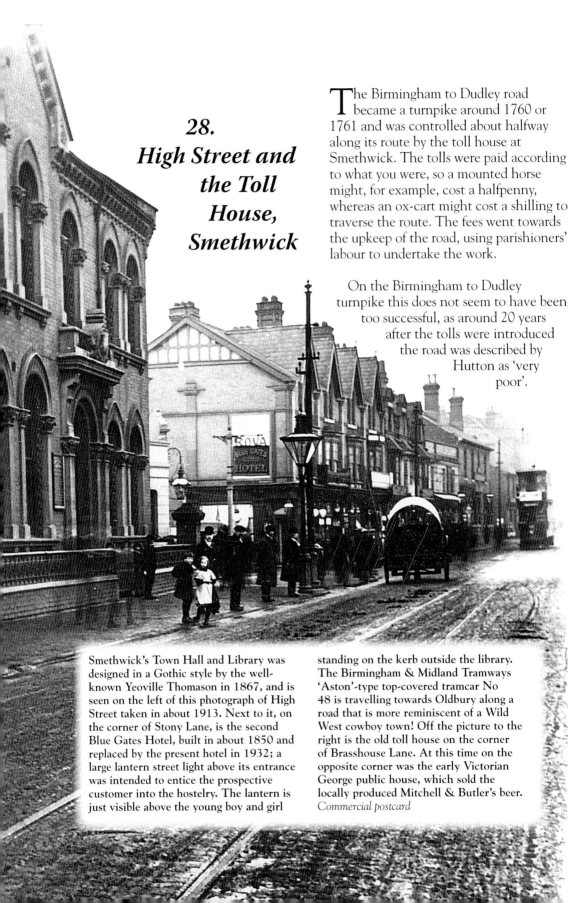

# 28.
# *High Street and the Toll House, Smethwick*

The Birmingham to Dudley road became a turnpike around 1760 or 1761 and was controlled about halfway along its route by the toll house at Smethwick. The tolls were paid according to what you were, so a mounted horse might, for example, cost a halfpenny, whereas an ox-cart might cost a shilling to traverse the route. The fees went towards the upkeep of the road, using parishioners' labour to undertake the work.

On the Birmingham to Dudley turnpike this does not seem to have been too successful, as around 20 years after the tolls were introduced the road was described by Hutton as 'very poor'.

Smethwick's Town Hall and Library was designed in a Gothic style by the well-known Yeoville Thomason in 1867, and is seen on the left of this photograph of High Street taken in about 1913. Next to it, on the corner of Stony Lane, is the second Blue Gates Hotel, built in about 1850 and replaced by the present hotel in 1932; a large lantern street light above its entrance was intended to entice the prospective customer into the hostelry. The lantern is just visible above the young boy and girl standing on the kerb outside the library. The Birmingham & Midland Tramways 'Aston'-type top-covered tramcar No 48 is travelling towards Oldbury along a road that is more reminiscent of a Wild West cowboy town! Off the picture to the right is the old toll house on the corner of Brasshouse Lane. At this time on the opposite corner was the early Victorian George public house, which sold the locally produced Mitchell & Butler's beer.
*Commercial postcard*

That it survived the wholesale demolition of the north side of the High Street is quite remarkable.

The original toll house was built on the corner of High Street and Brasshouse Lane by 1767, and was replaced in 1818 by the present Regency-styled building shown in the drawing. It has neat, almost church-like windows in a quite ordinary square-shaped house, except for the front extension where the toll office was located.

**The toll house was given its Smethwick Local History Society blue plaque in 2000, which signifies the building's historical importance.**

The three round-topped windows on the ground floor gave an all-round view along the High Street and enabled the toll-master to observe approaching travellers. Even in the 1820s, although Smethwick itself was still little more than a village, materials being carried to and from the ever-increasing number of foundries and machine shops, which were not being carried on the nearby Brindley and Telford canals of the Birmingham Canal Navigation, had to pass the toll house. As a result, it made a considerable profit for nearly the next 50 years.

Turnpikes were abolished in 1872, but by this time the original dispersed village of Smethwick had

SMETHWICK LOCAL HISTORY SOCIETY

Smethwick Cross
TOLLHOUSE
built circa 1820

This road was part of the
Birmingham, Wolverhampton
and Dudley Turnpike
1760 - 1876

2000

moved away from the old Bearwood Hill area and on to the High Street. Much of this movement was due to the reconstructed BCN main line of 1828, which attracted new commercial growth. The opening of the Birmingham, Wolverhampton & Stour Valley Railway in 1852 and the station at Rolfe Street continued to encourage the development in the High Street area. Gradually the more important buildings in Smethwick were built in High Street, with perhaps the best known being built directly opposite the toll house. These were the original Town Hall and Library, seen in the accompanying photographs.

*Right*: The view looking the other way towards Birmingham in 1985 shows the toll house, the 1932 Blue Gates public house and the library, but all the original properties that formed the north side of High Street have been demolished. This was done in 1981 in order to provide for the new Tollhouse Way bypass, although the traffic congestion on the emasculated High Street today is far worse than before the shops and houses that backed on to the main Birmingham to Wolverhampton railway line were demolished.

*Below*: On 25 January 2005 a lorry can be seen speeding along the dual-carriageway of Tollhouse Way only yards behind this lovely Regency 'gem'. *D. R. Harvey*

# 29.
# *The Manor House,*
# *West Bromwich*

The drawing shows the two projecting half-timbered rear wings, both of which date from about the 15th century. One of these originally contained the first-floor chapel, and can be recognised by its five-light leaded window with ogee headings. The western wing, however, had a much more prosaic function, being the site of the original Manor House kitchen.

The survival of this Manor House is truly amazing as in the early 1950s it was a derelict old house that was about to be demolished. It was 'touch and go' if, on acquisition, West Bromwich Corporation was going to restore this dilapidated and potentially expensive piece of real estate. It was only when W. Maurice Jones, a Worcester-based architect, looked carefully at the dreary old property that the existence of this hidden medieval 'gem' was discovered beneath its brick façade. Work was begun on the restoration of the building during 1957 and it was quickly acknowledged that parts of the Manor House dated from about 1290, with virtually nothing added to it after the 16th century.

Dendrochronology has revealed that some of the original timbers used in its construction were felled in 1275. In other words, the building was complete and most of it more than 200 years old by the time William Shakespeare wrote The Two Gentlemen of Verona, one of his earliest plays dating from the same year as the Spanish Armada – 1588! Yet for well over a century it was known locally in the Stone Cross area as the 'Old Hall' and all but ignored.

The house was built by the Devereaux and de Marnham families, related through two sisters who were daughters of William Fitz-Wido, the Lord of the Manor. Sara married a Walter Devereux and the younger Margaret married Richard de Marnham, and for the next 200 years the Manor House was kept in the family. Originally the building consisted of little more than the Great Hall, but by 1450 the north and south cross wings had been added. It had passed into the ownership of the Stanley family by 1515, and they built the gatehouse, improved the Great Hall and had their own chapel constructed. The house subsequently went through the ownership of a number of wealthy local worthies, including the Clarke family, who created a kitchen garden and clad the old timber framing in brick so that it looked 'modern' to Georgian eyes.

After being sold in 1823, the house went into what appeared to be terminal decline, initially being turned into a multi-occupancy dwelling and, by the 1880s, into a tenement with rooms to let. Its restoration began in 1957 after a long period of uncertainty, and it was then that the long-forgotten moat, which forms a horseshoe shape around the rear of the extensive property, was dug out, and this is shown on the right of the drawing.

Part of the funding of the restoration, which cost £24,500, was provided by the then Birmingham

*Right:* By 1950 the Manor House looked ready for demolition. Research on what looked like a delapidated Georgian house, plus the interest of local historians began to prevail and it was soon shown that it was a lot more than just an ugly eyesore.

based Ansells Brewery on the understanding that it would become a working building once again and not just a lifeless museum piece. As a result, by the end of 1960 the Manor House became a restaurant and public house, a role it continues to play today, although since 1986 it has been excellently managed by the Wolverhampton & Dudley Breweries, better known as Banks's.

Since the original restoration a considerable amount of remedial work was undertaken on the Manor House in the early 1980s to replace rotten wood, and today this hidden building is still 'undersold' as regards its importance to the local community and to West Bromwich in general. This is a great pity, as this remarkable survivor of probably 700 years ago would be a star tourist attraction in Stratford-upon-Avon and be regarded as a real treasure, whereas although immaculately maintained it is underrated as both a historic building and as a pub of potential great age. Where else could one drink in a pub even older than the Greyhound in Bilston (qv)?

The entrance to the Manor House is through a timber-framed Elizabethan gatehouse with rather delightful wooden-framed decorations at the jettied first-floor level, as seen in this January 2005 view. The central opening leads into a small courtyard, with the old half-timbered chapel to the right up a flight of stone steps, as seen in the second photograph. To the left in the courtyard is the entrance to the main part of the licensed premises, but originally this beautifully restored space was the early-14th-century Great Hall, probably built for William de Marnham, by then the direct-line inheritor of the Lord of the Manor title. This large hall is splendidly authentic, especially with its fine restored timber roof and large crucks that carry the columns capped with carved capitals. Set into the south side of the hall is a mezzanine reached by a set of stone steps that lead into an ante-room then, by way of a screen passage, to a raised dais with a canopy of honour. Underneath this, in almost a floor-level undercroft, is the well hidden bar, while at the high-table end of the hall, beneath a slightly later rectangular Tudor bay window, is the present-day food serving area. *Both D. R. Harvey*

*Above:* This Victorian postcard shows that the Market Place looks much the same today, with the Memorial Clock being the focus of attention. This monument was funded by the Friendly Societies of Willenhall and was unveiled on 10 May 1892 in memory of Dr Joseph Tonks. The whole memorial cost £250 and was designed by a Mr Boddis, a Birmingham stonemason. It was beautifully restored to full working order in 1979. Dr Tonks was a local man who graduated as a member of the Royal College of Surgeons in 1879 and went back to his home town, where he gained a reputation for giving his services free of charge to the needy of the town. His health never recovered following a ballooning accident at the Willenhall horticultural show of 1888, in which he badly injured his leg and shoulder when the balloon, its basket and a Lieutenant Lampriere broke free from its mooring ropes with the unfortunate doctor inside the basket as a local celebrity passenger. Although Dr Tonks made a sort of recovery, his health was permanently damaged and he died within three years, just short of his 36th birthday. *Commercial postcard*

*Left and above right:* The Victorian photograph of Ye Old Bell Inn shows the notice stating that it was 'established in 1680' and that it sells wines and spirits. In view of its then somewhat run-down state it is surprising that it is still with us and thriving in the 21st century! No 33 is on the right behind the iron railings, and at this time had a tree growing in the front garden. *Jonathan Lewis*

# 30.
# *Willenhall Market Place*

Today Willenhall is a suburb of Wolverhampton, but it has a long, proud history of its own, dating back to the Domesday Book when it was recorded as 'Winehale'. The locksmiths arrived here in the 16th century and developed a thriving domestic industry until its gradual decline after the founding of the first factory in the late 18th century. Today Willenhall is still the most important lock-making centre in the United Kingdom. The Josiah Parkes Company was founded in 1840 and became the manufacturer of Union Locks in 1896. The company rapidly became the largest lock-maker in the town, while the future of the company was assured with the introduction of cylinder locks in 1911. The lock-making companies that

*Below:* The photograph taken in January 2005 shows the present-day pedestrianised Market Place from the other, New Road, end. The two lovingly restored three-storey blocks, which date from 1792, contain a General Store at the near end, and a remarkably traditional ironmonger at the far corner of the Market Place; the latter has galvanised buckets, bins, tools and general household goods in a display that would do justice in the Black Country Living Museum in Dudley, and even has 'that ironmonger's smell'! The Tonks Memorial Clock is visible beyond.
*D. R. Harvey*

were attracted to the town were J. Legge, which specialised in door locks and lock furniture, and Henry Squire, which was founded in 1780 at New Invention and became best known for its padlocks, as well as other manufacturers including William Pinson, Enoch Pinson, Gibbons, Shepherds and Abel Fletchers. The American Yale lock company came to the town in 1929 when it took over an existing lock-maker and introduced the mass-produced pin tumbler lock. Even today there are about 15 locksmiths in Willenhall and the town has the National Lock Museum in New Road; opened in 1986, it is administered by the Black Country Living Museum.

Only nine years after St Giles, in Walsall Street, became the Parish Church, the town barely survived a terrible cholera epidemic in 1849, which in three months killed 292 people. The growth of the town began as it recovered from the epidemic and the old Market Place was redeveloped. It is this part of Willenhall that qualifies as a 'hidden gem', for although it comprises the main street through the town, it is to the north of the main B4464 road between Wolverhampton and Walsall. Lying directly opposite Bilston Street and Rose Hill, where the Georgian Dale House is located, the area comprising the Market Place and Cross Street is an undervalued and almost unspoilt 18th-and-19th-century town centre. Many of the 'gems' in the Market Place are pre-Victorian. No 33, an asymmetrically fronted house, is set back from the Bell Inn and

dates from 1756. This is a real nugget of an earlier architectural style, and while not as perfectly proportioned as earlier Georgian buildings, it represents a surviving town house owned by a wealthy merchant.

He was William Aston, who was a 'chapman', a general dealer primarily in metal, in this case for the local lock-manufacturing industry. Aston came from nearby Sneyd and owned the house on the other side of the Bell Inn. This property was used as a warehouse on the ground floor, to store his metals, while on the first floor was the accommodation for his servants. Between the two properties is the even older Bell Inn, a converted farm building parts of which are the oldest structures in Willenhall. The pub dates from its rebuilding in

1660, having partially survived a fire that had recently swept through the town; at the rear of the building there are timbers that were part of the original structure and have been dated to about 1580.

What makes this part of Willenhall even more interesting is that most of the buildings were largely constructed between about 1850 and 1900, and the result is an almost undisturbed 'time capsule'. If the Market Place was seen in a period drama production on television, with careful editing it could almost be a made-to-measure outside production set. It is not even as though any of the individual buildings themselves have any architectural merit, but together they form a delightful area that is better than the sum of its parts.

Today the Market Place area of Willenhall is a real 'voyage of discovery' and is well worth its conservation status, but it does seem a shame that this important Black Country town has such an underused asset.

*Left:* The detailed drawing was made from outside the Bell Inn looking back to New Road and the distant Dale House. It shows the size of the square with the rest of the three-storied premises going into Cross Street on the left with the ironmonger's shop behind the Tonks Memorial Clock. The tall turreted building at the far end of the Market Place is the HSBC Bank, which was built on the corner of New Road for the Metropolitan Bank around the last decade of Queen Victoria's reign. New Road got its name when it was opened in 1818 to improve access to Wolverhampton. On the right-hand side of the Market Place is another block of three-storey 18th-century shops that is slightly older than the one containing the ironmongers. The drawing really captures the well-preserved 'Dickensian' Market Place, and if all the shop fronts could be restored to the same standard as those described earlier, Willenhall could certainly become a real-life film set!

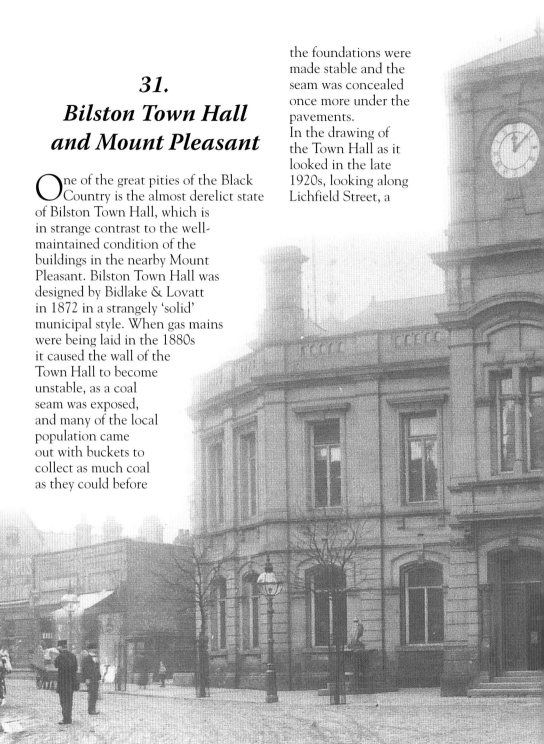

# 31.
# Bilston Town Hall and Mount Pleasant

One of the great pities of the Black Country is the almost derelict state of Bilston Town Hall, which is in strange contrast to the well-maintained condition of the buildings in the nearby Mount Pleasant. Bilston Town Hall was designed by Bidlake & Lovatt in 1872 in a strangely 'solid' municipal style. When gas mains were being laid in the 1880s it caused the wall of the Town Hall to become unstable, as a coal seam was exposed, and many of the local population came out with buckets to collect as much coal as they could before the foundations were made stable and the seam was concealed once more under the pavements.

In the drawing of the Town Hall as it looked in the late 1920s, looking along Lichfield Street, a

Wolverhampton Corporation tramcar is on its way back to its home town. Since through running had been agreed with the Wolverhampton District Company in 1905, dual-equipped trams such as No 22, constructed by G. F. Milnes in early 1904, were operating using the overhead wiring. The large photograph was taken in 1898, only 25 years after the impressive Town Hall was built on the corner of Lichfield Street and Church Street, and a Wolverhampton Tramways Company horse tram clops up the hill in Lichfield Street towards the distant junction with Mount Pleasant when working on the Moxley to Wolverhampton service. This standard gauge (4ft 8½in) tramcar had been built by Falcon in Loughborough in 1892, and this is possibly the only known photograph of a horse tram in Bilston. Note the appalling state of the road surface, which even in the centre of a town the size of Bilston, in the late-Victorian period, was a horrendous mixture of mud and horse manure, reminding one of how conditions improved after mechanised transport replaced horses.

*D. R. Harvey collection*

*Below:* The bunting and the flags are out in June 1953 to celebrate the Coronation of HM Queen Elizabeth II, and this certainly helps to brighten up the town in the early post-war years of rationing, long hours for poor wages, and a general drabness that seemed prevalent at the time. The Georgian White Rose pub on the left even has a large photograph of the Queen over a first-floor window. There were hardly any new cars to brighten up the roads as the 'export or bust' policy meant that cars from 'The Austin' were built for export. Thus it is that the only car on the road is a 1938 Morris Eight, which looks as if it has seen better days. *Commercial postcard*

*Top right:* The present-day photograph, taken in December 2004, shows the Town Hall to be much cleaner and apparently in good order. Unfortunately at the time of the photograph it was boarded up and awaiting some sort of restoration package, which will hopefully restore the building to its rightful place as one of the 'gems' of the Black Country.

*Middle right:* In the distance of the 2004 photograph of the Town Hall can be seen the collection of elegant early-19th-century buildings that cluster around Mount Pleasant. On the corner is a Classically styled three-storey Regency town house, while in Mount Pleasant itself is a row of delightful Regency houses.

*Bottom right:* On the opposite corner, taken in April 2007 the former Parsonage, designed by Francis Goodwin in about 1830. It was built with a charming three-bay design and prominent pilasters, and after a period of being unloved has recently been restored to its former glory. Behind the Parsonage, St Leonard's Church, which was begun in 1825 and also designed by Francis Goodwin in a nicely plain Classical style with well-proportioned round-arched nave windows.
*All D. R. Harvey*

# 32.
# *Red House Cone, Audnam, Amblecote*

The Stuart Crystal Red House glass cone is the sole survivor of the many built in the Stourbridge area. It was built in the period between 1788 and 1794 by Richard Bradley, a local industrialist, and the location between locks 12 and 13 on the Stourbridge Canal was chosen to make use of the newly constructed waterway. The Stourbridge Canal, work on which had begun after its Parliamentary Act had been passed in 1776, was a vital link to the outside world for the glass industry in the Stourbridge, Audnam and Brierley Hill triangle.

Unlike many other Black Country canals, the Stourbridge retained its commercial goods traffic until Nationalisation in

1948, after which it quickly fell into disrepair and had become unnavigable by the mid-1950s. Volunteer labour from the Staffs & Worcester Society, formed in 1964, took three years to re-open the canal, and the two locks adjacent to the glass cone are part of the flight known as the 'Stourbridge Sixteen', which raise the Canal some 148 feet between Wordsley Junction and Leys Junction.

The Red House Cone was used for glass-making from the mid-1790s until 1936,

*Right:* **This February 2005 view from the Double Lock Cottage looking down the 'Stourbridge Sixteen' flight of locks illustrates just how much the Red House Cone dominated the sky-line over the Audnam and Wordsley area. It also shows the preserved timber warehouse, known as 'Dadford's Shed' after Thomas Dadford Jnr, who was the canal engineer.** *D. R. Harvey*

when production was moved across the main road to factory-type premises in Vine Street. The glass cone was both a workplace and a chimney, with the glass-blowers working at ground level, while in the centre and above the workers was the 23-foot-diameter furnace with 12 melting ovens radiating from it. It was here that the metal or molten glass was melted and gathered by the glass-blowers for shaping. The shape of the cone drew

the fire of the furnace so effectively that temperatures reached 1,400°C, which was necessary to melt the glass. Today the Stuart Crystal glass cone is the best preserved of only four that survive in the rest of the country. At around 90 feet high and 60 feet wide at the base, this monster of brick can hardly be termed a 'hidden gem', but remembering its historical significance and the sheer beauty of the 'beast', this last remaining

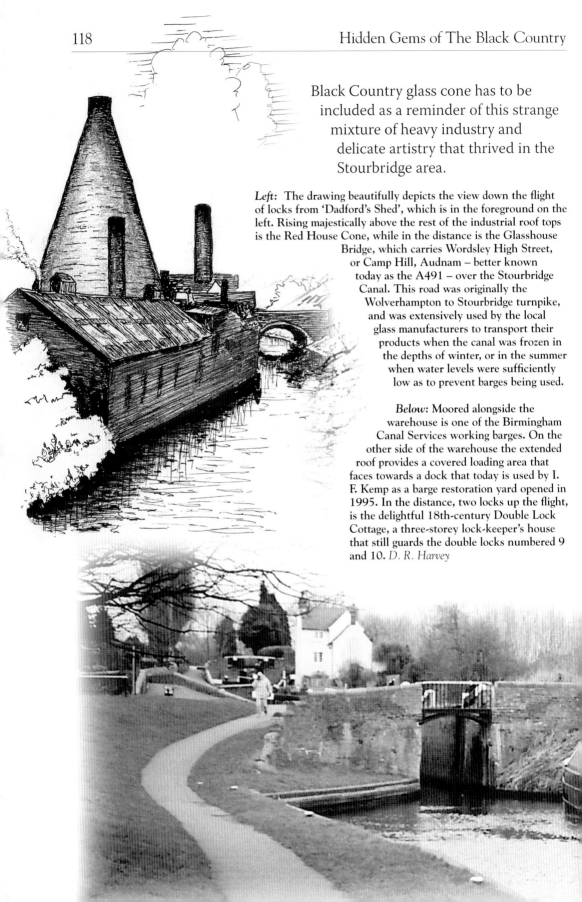

Black Country glass cone has to be included as a reminder of this strange mixture of heavy industry and delicate artistry that thrived in the Stourbridge area.

*Left:* The drawing beautifully depicts the view down the flight of locks from 'Dadford's Shed', which is in the foreground on the left. Rising majestically above the rest of the industrial roof tops is the Red House Cone, while in the distance is the Glasshouse Bridge, which carries Wordsley High Street, or Camp Hill, Audnam – better known today as the A491 – over the Stourbridge Canal. This road was originally the Wolverhampton to Stourbridge turnpike, and was extensively used by the local glass manufacturers to transport their products when the canal was frozen in the depths of winter, or in the summer when water levels were sufficiently low as to prevent barges being used.

*Below:* Moored alongside the warehouse is one of the Birmingham Canal Services working barges. On the other side of the warehouse the extended roof provides a covered loading area that faces towards a dock that today is used by I. F. Kemp as a barge restoration yard opened in 1995. In the distance, two locks up the flight, is the delightful 18th-century Double Lock Cottage, a three-storey lock-keeper's house that still guards the double locks numbered 9 and 10. *D. R. Harvey*

The Red House Cone was classified as a Grade II listed building in 1966 and serious work on its restoration began in 1982. The Red House Glassworks Working Museum was set up just two years later and the Cone obtained Grade II* status in 1999. This was just as well, since Stuart Crystal had been taken over by Waterford Wedgwood in 1995 and the nearby factory in Vine Street was closed with the loss of 220 jobs, effectively marking the end of industrial glass-making in the Stourbridge area.

In 2001 Dudley MBC obtained funding from Advantage West Midlands, the Heritage Lottery, the European Development Fund, English Heritage and Stuart Crystal totalling £1.375 million to restore the Red House Cone, turning it back into a real 'not so hidden gem' of the Black Country.

*Above right:* This view of the front of the cone from the main road entrance dates from June 1985, and at that time the place was a working museum and had not been sanitised into the visitor attraction that it is today; the outbuildings had not been restored, and it gave the visitor much more of a feel for the conditions when it had been a dirty, polluting factory, belching out smoke from both the top and the bottom of the cone. It was not then the idealised historical monument.
*D. R. Harvey*

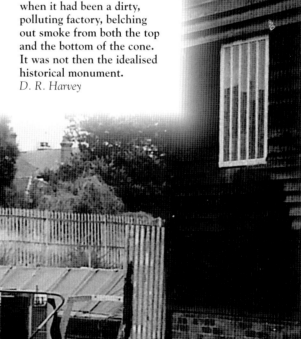

## 33.
## *The Old Swan, Netherton and The Vine, Brierley Hill*

Throughout the Black Country beer-making was a thriving industry and most individual public houses brewed their own beers in the back yards where there was a small brewhouse, pronounced 'brewus' in the Black Country. Because of the chain-makers, nail-makers, glass-blowers and both the small and large iron and steel foundries that had grown up throughout the Black Country to exploit the local reserves of coal, iron ore, limestone and sand, there was a desperate need to slake the thirst of the men. They worked in front of roaring furnaces where temperatures of 1,400ºC were required to melt the iron, steel or glass, so beer-drinking became a necessity rather than a leisure activity. The local water supply was frequently of a dubious quality, being infected with typhoid or cholera bacteria, so beer, which had been boiled in the brewing process, was the best way to stop dehydration and disease at the furnace door.

So it was that public houses began to brew their own beer, and nearby factories would employ 'pot-boys' to collect pitchers of beer all day to take to the sweating foundrymen. Pubs that brewed their own beer were gradually taken over, which meant that by the early 1970s there were just four home-brew pubs, the most famous being The Old Swan, in Netherton. This pub was better known at the time as 'Ma Pardoe's' after Doris Pardoe, who was the landlady from the 1930s until her death in 1984.

The Old Swan, seen here in February 2005, has been largely unchanged since 1863, with its enamel-plate white swan ceiling, reflecting the pub's original name, and mirrored wooden back bar furniture. With its 'Pure Home Brewd Ales' notice emblazoned across the front, the pub has survived to be one of the best-known real ale 'boozers' in the Black Country.
The strange statue on the left is of the famous Windmill 'Endian', one Josey Darby, who latterly was the publican of the Albion in Stone Street, Dudley. In the 1890s Darby was the World Champion of a sport that has all but died out today – Spring Jumping – and Darby's feats were truly remarkable. He achieved a backward spring jump of almost 13 feet, jumping the length of a snooker table from a standing start. Also, and surely most remarkably, he became the first man since Jesus to walk on water. This was done when he jumped across a wide canal in two bounds, the second one using the surface of the water as a springboard! So here is his statue looking as though he is about to make another one of his astonishing spring jumps straight into the bar of The Old Swan. *D. R. Harvey*

The Black Country breweries fared little better than their Birmingham counterparts, though they survived longer. While Wolverhampton & Dudley Breweries continues to thrive and grow with its Campaign for Real Ale (CAMRA)-recommended real ales, three smaller breweries, J. P. Simpkiss, Edwin Holdens and Daniel Batham, all survived and to some extent thrived in the revival of hand-pumped beers encouraged by CAMRA, which was established in 1971. Simpkiss, based in Brettell Lane, brewed its last pint in 1985, having been taken over by Greenall Whitley, although the brew lives on, being produced by the Enville Brewery of Stourbridge. Holdens is based in Woodsetton at the Park Inn Brewery, and produces a wide range of excellent real ales. Finally, at the Beacon Hotel in Sedgley, the Sarah Hughes Brewery, which re-opened in 1987 after a closure of 30 years, now supplies more than 500 outlets with its four different

brews. However, it is with the third of the surviving major independent brewers that this section is concerned.

Daniel Batham first established a brewery in Netherton quite near to the aforementioned White Swan, but took over the public house and adjacent brewery of the Worcester Brewing & Malting Company in Delph Road, Brierley Hill, in 1905. The drawing shows The Vine in Delph Road with, emblazoned across its façade, the Shakespearian quotation 'Blessing of your heart, you brew good ale' from Act III, Sc I of The Two Gentlemen of Verona, when Launce refers slightly strangely to the quotation as a quotation! The pub is known locally as 'the Bull and Bladder' and has a most colourful frontage behind which is a multi-roomed public house, with coal fires and memorabilia connected with Batham's beers.

Both of these well-known public houses are to be found in the annual nationwide CAMRA guide. While well-known in the West Midlands and scarcely 'hidden', perhaps their fame is unjustifiably not quite as widespread outside the area, so go and find these two 'gems' and enjoy their individually unique qualities.

*Below:* The Vine is seen in this 2005 picture of the famous public house, while the view up the hill in Delph Road *(right)* reveals the Delph Brewery next door, which was established in 1877 before Daniel Batham took over the site. *Both D. R. Harvey*

## 34.
## The Molineux
## Hotel and
## Giffard House,
## Wolverhampton

The Grade II* listed Molineux Hotel has led a somewhat chequered career, and in recent years has been a gaunt and derelict shell hidden behind the high parapet wall of St Peter's Ringway. It was built as a wonderful Georgian town house in the 1720s, then in the late 1740s it came into the ownership of Benjamin Molineux, whose family were wealthy ironmongers and merchants. When built, Molineux House was situated at the edge of the growing Georgian town of Wolverhampton, but despite being swallowed up by the Regency housing along Tettenhall Road (qv) and the nearby Whitmore Reans, the house still occupied a commanding site with vistas to the west. This five-bay, three-storey building, with additional Georgian wings and a Victorian turret, remained with the Molineux family until it was bought in 1860 by O. E. McGregor, a baker and confectioner. The South Staffordshire Industrial & Fine Art Exhibition was held in the house and gardens in 1869, and during the following year it became the Molineux Hotel.

The grounds behind the house became pleasure gardens and were used for sporting events, the most popular being the then 'new-fangled' cycle races. Yet it was here that Wolverhampton Wanderers played their first games, having turned professional in 1888 and becoming one of the 12 founder members of the Football League. Originally the football club had been formed by a group of schoolteachers from St Luke's, Blakenhall, but they moved to their new ground about the time that they were admitted to the new Football League. Behind the hotel the club built their new football ground, which is today the famous Molineux Stadium. However, while the football ground has been transformed by the investments of the Hayward family since 1991, the old hotel, separated from the town by the Ring Road, lay derelict for a quarter of a century, having closed in 1979.

Even comments by HRH The Prince of Wales failed to stir any organisation into more than expressing a desire that something should be done to save the building. A Wolverhampton property developer, Peter Maddox, bought the hotel with a view to converting it into – well, anything really, offices, hotel, conference centre and hotel… But as the building became more and more neglected, the interior gutted and burned out, and the tower looking in danger of collapse, any attempts to restore the building with a view to making it an economically viable proposition also collapsed! The drawing shows the building in the summer of 2004, surrounded by fencing and surmounted by cranes, but this was the beginning of the Molineux's renaissance. The regional development agency, Advantage West Midlands, has funded the external restoration of the building by raising £1.5 million for the initial phase. This will include rebuilding all the external walls, providing a new roof and renewing the floors, and all in 77 weeks. In the future a second grant will be made to restore the plasterwork, rebuild the impressive central main staircase and make the building ready for – well, anyone who can find a suitable use for it, perhaps even a hotel again…

by the brewers W. Butler & Co and was used as a public house until the construction of the Ring Road made it impossible to remain financially viable as the new road separated it from the town centre. *J. H. Hughes collection*

*Below:* This July 1984 photograph shows how being empty for only five years had affected the building. Two of the four almost 150-foot-tall floodlight pylons at the Molineux ground, erected in 1957, are visible behind the already derelict Georgian building. *D. R. Harvey*

*Above:* The Victorian photograph shows the attractive hotchpotch of 18th-century buildings that made up the front of the well-maintained Molineux Hotel. It is often forgotten that from 1870 for more than 70 years the Molineux was the meeting place and function house for the 'great and good' of Wolverhampton, through the Victorian and Edwardian period right up to the beginning of the Second World War. Latterly it was owned

The church of St Peter & St Paul is actually built into the rear of the house; it was begun in 1826, but a century later it was looking considerably down at heel. In 1989 the Grade II* listed building was lovingly restored together with the church, and the drawing shows the combined Giffard House and church in this refurbished condition. As it is located within full view of the Molineux Hotel, it should provide some inspiration for what a carefully restored building could look like.

Giffard House dates from 1728 and is a characteristic early-Georgian brick-built town house with two and a half storeys and five bays. It was built by a Francis Smith of Warwick for Peter Giffard of Chillington, a well-known local Roman Catholic activist, who handed the house over to the local Roman Catholic authorities in 1734 when it was used as a Mass House. Hidden within what looked like a prosperous merchant's house was a chapel for the local Catholics to worship in during a time when Catholicism was a dangerous religion to be following.

*Below*: Outside Giffard House in 1928 single-deck trolleybus UK 626, a Tilling-Stevens TS6 with a 36-seater Dodson body, picks up a passenger in Wulfruna Street when on its way out of the town along Stafford Road to Fordhouses, while a Ford A-type 15cwt light lorry speeds along North Street. *D. R. Harvey collection*

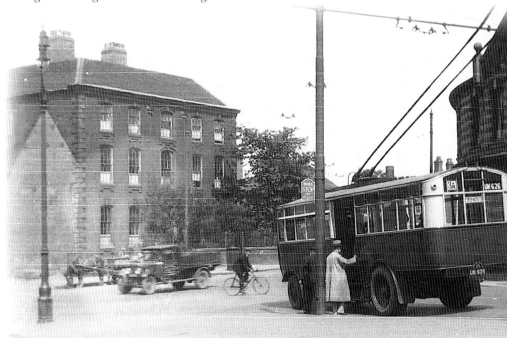

# 35. Council House, Oldbury

The last remnant of Victorian civic pride to survive the ravages of neglect and subsequent demolition to create a sort of strangely 'buildingless' central Oldbury is the old Council House. This prominent municipal building was built to the design of the architects Wood and Kendrick in an attractive red brick with dressings and facings in terracotta. The style of the building was an odd mixture of Gothic-cum-Stuart superimposed on a Renaissance structure that was so favoured in the late 19th century as a symbol of Victorian 'Civic Pride'. It was even built with a rounded turret on the corner of Halesowen Street and Freeth Street, surmounted by a tower with a somewhat squat spire that fails to soar upwards! The main entrance doorway in Freeth Street is a rather attractive affair, beyond which is a splendid curved staircase leading to the old Council Chamber and large office rooms.

The Cenotaph, built in the Market Place in front of the Town Hall, was unveiled on 4 November 1926 by General Sir Ian Hamilton, who had been the General Commander of the British Expeditionary Force during the ill-fated 1915 Gallipoli campaign in the Dardanelles. Today it is inscribed with the updated wording

'IN MEMORY OF THE MEN OF OLDBURY WHO FELL IN THE GREAT WARS 1914-1918 AND 1939-1945'.

*Left*: The Town Hall and the Council House beyond it are seen in this 1970 photograph. Originally known as the People's Hall, the Town Hall was later also known as the Public Hall before adopting the more usual name. It was rather an uninspired building, especially when compared to the later Council House, looking rather like a Victorian Board School with three large round-topped two-storey windows on each of the Market Place and Temperance Street sides. It was demolished to be replaced by the Savacentre superstore, which opened in October 1980, but fortunately the adjoining Council House was saved. *J. Spooner, courtesy T. Daniels*

*Left*: Until the new Sandwell Council House was built in 1991 opposite the by then preserved earlier Council House, the latter still dominated the centre of the town. Today the situation has been totally reversed. This 2006 photograph of the Market Place shows just how much the new building dominates the centre of Oldbury, separated from the old building by the now pedestrianised Freeth Street. The Cenotaph has been moved slightly in order to allow better access for the annual Festival of Remembrance in November. Behind it, abutted by the edge of the huge Savacentre store, is the comforting red brick of the old Council House, today protected by a wide paved and landscaped area. *D. R. Harvey*

*Left*: This December 1982 view shows the old 19th-century retail premises opposite the Council House. *D. R. Harvey*

# 36.
# *Chapel Ash and Tettenhall Road, Wolverhampton*

The Chapel Ash area of Wolverhampton grew up around the beginning of the 19th century where a three-way road junction had developed. The main route through Chapel Ash was the important turnpike road to the north-west leading to the nearby village of Tettenhall. Subsequently improved in the early 1800s by the Wolverhampton Turnpike Trust, who largely ignored the advice of Thomas Telford, this, the present-day A41, links to the A5.

In the 2006 drawing the street furniture, traffic lights and road layout somewhat mask the majority of the 19th-century buildings that have managed to survive, including Westbourne Place itself. Nowadays, the whole of the Chapel Ash junction seems much smaller and therefore more congested than when the electric trams were introduced more than 100 years ago, and this complicated five-way junction struggles to cope with today's traffic conditions as one of Wolverhampton's most congested crossroads.

The latter, which was rebuilt and realigned by Telford, follows the line of the Roman Watling Street and was designed to take the intrepid Georgian stagecoach traveller to Shrewsbury, Llangollen and through North Wales and beyond Snowdonia to Holyhead in Anglesey. The second road leading due west from Chapel Ash was Compton Road, which in turn led through the nearby Shropshire countryside to Bridgnorth. A third, more minor road led to the medieval Merridale Farm and to villages such as Trysull in the Smestow Valley. Chapel Ash quickly developed during the post-Napoleonic War and Regency period so that by the time of Queen Victoria's accession the area had become Wolverhampton's first real suburb. Today it is hard to believe that the Chapel Ash area was not originally part of Wolverhampton, as it is almost indistinguishable from the present-day city centre.

Located in the fork of Tettenhall Road and Compton Road is the delightful Regency-built Westbourne Place, which for many years in the 19th century served as a doctor's surgery. As Chapel Ash

became more important, so did the need to link it with Wolverhampton, and the Wolverhampton Tramway Company opened a horse tram route on 1 May 1878, charging 2d for the 12-minute journey to Newbridge at the Staffordshire & Worcester Canal bridge that formed the boundary between Wolverhampton CBC and Tettenhall UDC.

*Main picture:* This photograph dates from about 1903, as electric tramcar No 16 is going to Tettenhall, and this service was only opened on 13 September 1902, exactly three months after the opening of the new electric tram service to Newbridge. One unusual aspect of electric tramcar operation in Wolverhampton was the lack of overhead wiring. It was the residents of the tree-lined Tettenhall Road who were instrumental in objecting to an electric tramway with the usual 'unsightly' overhead. As a result, together with the influence of Alderman Charles Mander, the Lorain Surface Contact system was introduced in the town. If it wasn't particularly successful, it certainly left everywhere free of overhead wires, enabling the tram routes to retain their uncluttered skyline. On the right of this early Edwardian photograph the suburban shops include Godsell's the chemist, which stands on the corner of Bath Road, leading to Banks's brewery. *D. R. Harvey collection*

Horse-drawn carriages and cabs became so popular around this time for the well-to-do residents of Compton and Tettenhall Roads that a Hackney carriage drivers' shelter was built in front of Westbourne Place alongside a large stone horse trough.

In the background of the 1903 photograph, Tettenhall Road is already lined with mature elm, lime and plane trees stretching down the hill to the Halfway House Inn. This part of Tettenhall Road was, and fortunately still is today, lined with some of the most exquisite terraced housing in Wolverhampton. The start of these houses can be seen in the Chapel Ash drawing, and the second sketch (above right) shows these late-Regency terraces in more detail. Tettenhall Road's development continued throughout the 1830s and early 1840s, and this period is reflected in the name plaques mounted

on the elegant houses and terraced blocks along the southern side, with Palmerston Place and the terraces of Osborne, Lansdowne, Blenheim, Oakland and Peel gracing the road.

*Above:* **A panoramic view of the south side of Tettenhall Road.**

*Right:* This view of Tettenhall Road's balconied Regency houses in the autumn of 2004 reveals just what an attractive row of buildings they are. No 5 Tettenhall Road, in the block originally named Eagle Terrace, was occupied between 1866 and his death in 1909 by the well-known local botanist and geologist John Frazer, whose collection of more than ten thousand items was donated to Wolverhampton's Art Gallery and Museum. *D. R. Harvey*

*Below:* Finally, by way of contrast, here is another 'hidden gem' located in Lovatt Street off Chapel Ash, which today is a dead-end leading to Banks's Park Brewery, but which in Edwardian times linked Chapel Ash to Bath Road and the lodge entrance to West Park. Here there is the remnant of a terrace of early artisans' housing, which has been restored and is used today as offices. Why they are so interesting is debatable, except that they highlight the difference between the housing of the wealthy owners of the nearby Regency terraces on Tettenhall Road with those of clerks and office staff who might have been able to afford Lovatt Street's terraces. *D. R. Harvey*

# 37. Remnants of old Halesowen

The town of Halesowen is located at the south-west of the Black Country in the valley of the meandering infant River Stour and is adjacent to the southernmost outcrops of the Carboniferous Coal Measures. Halesowen nestles between the bottom of the escarpment of the Birmingham Plateau and the Clent Hills, so whichever way one leaves the town one has to go up hill! Its location also means that the juxtaposition of the rural and the urban are never far away. The village of Halas was granted by King Henry II to the Prince of Wales, David ap Owen, in 1177, thus becoming Halas or, later, Hales Owen, and this spelling of the town's name survived until at least the 1930s.

Given borough status by the Abbot of Halesowen in 1232, the tiny village became known for its medieval weaving and cloth-fulling domestic industries. The manor passed into the ownership of the Lyttleton family, who subsequently built the nearby Hagley Hall; the most famous member of the family today is

*Left:* Dominating the town is the Parish Church of St John the Baptist, whose tower can be seen from all around the town. A religious structure has stood on this site since Saxon times, though nothing of this original wooden structure survived the Norman rebuilding. The drawing of the Parish Church represents the view from High Street in about 1910, and shows a Perpendicular Gothic-style church dating mainly from around the 14th and 15th centuries. This masks a lot of surviving Norman walls, arches, windows and doorways from the 12th-century structure, which was as large as the present church. Although partially rebuilt for its re-opening in 1884, much of the medieval and Norman fabric surprisingly survived this late-Victorian refurbishment. The original tower collapsed in the late 14th century and was unusually located to rise up from the middle of the nave at the west end of the church. The local novelist Francis Brett Young (1884-1954) described the Parish Church of St John the Baptist as 'our little cathedral', which perfectly describes this lovely looking church.

the jazz trumpeter and humorist Humphrey Lyttleton.

The exposure of coal on the western flank of the Stour Valley transformed the market village into a Georgian town, which rapidly became a post-Industrial Revolution centre for nail-making.

*Below:* The Parish Church is built in lovely soft red Hasbury sandstone, and the tower, with its tall grey spire, is unique in English church architecture. *D. R. Harvey*

This was an awful industry and of the Halesowen of 1844 it was written by an anonymous writer that 'In the midst of God's bounty and loveliness stalks the curse of poverty.

The whole population of this bounteous region being, without distinction of sex, nailors, a name at once description of all poverty and wretchedness.' The town has been served by canals and railways with limited success over the years and is now totally reliant on the congested roads and the nearby M5, where the road sign at Junction 3 fails to mention Halesowen at all!

Standing next to the church is the old Market Cross, which was moved to this site from the Cornbow after being blown down in a gale, while almost opposite in nearby Church Lane, formerly Dog Lane, are the surviving half-timbered White Friars Cottages. These date from about 1325 and were originally built as religious premises. Only 24 years after they were built, the first of four epidemics of the Black Death struck the village and the associated hamlets in the parish with devastating results.

*Above:* White Friars Cottages, looking from opposite the church down into the steeply incised valley of the River Stour. Just visible in the valley bottom of Church Lane, in the delightfully named Rumbow, is another medieval half-timbered cottage. D. R. Harvey

In the 1960s, Halesowen's town centre was scandalously and unnecessarily gutted, with character-rich Georgian buildings being replaced with horrendously anonymous concrete-framed premises. Strangely, for a town of this size, there are very few surviving photographs of these buildings in and around High Street. Only a comparatively small number of the really old buildings were left after this savage redevelopment, a number of which are shown in the photograph of High Street, but fortunately those which do survive capture the way the town used to look.

*Left:* The three-storey building in High Street used to belong to the Tennent family, who were primarily dispensing chemists, but gradually the premises became more famous as a railway model shop, with its successor still in existence at Hasbury. For many years, until taken over and refurbished by the present occupants, the upper storey windows were protected by barbed wire, put in place for the impending invasion by German forces in the summer of 1940! D. R. Harvey

# 38.
## Stourbridge town centre

J ust occasionally there is a street corner tucked away somewhere or a collection of apparently disparately styled buildings located next to each other that stand out as something just a little different. Stourbridge has just that sort of location, and this section undertakesa short tour of it, radiating from the Town Clock. In the middle of the town, where High Street meets Lower High Street and is crossed by Coventry Street to the east and Crown Lane and Market Street to the west, is the Town Clock, which appears in the drawing and several of the photographs. The

Town Clock was erected in 1857 to the designs of William Millward, the Council's resident engineer, and constructed at the Stourbridge Ironworks of John Bradley & Co. It features two round faces in an octagonal frame on top of an attractively fluted cast-iron column. Behind this focal point on the corner of High Street and Market Street is the former Market Hall. The façade dates from 1827 and, as the drawing reveals, it has three bays with four columns going from ground level to the flat face of the roof. The rest of the building is part of the Crown Centre shopping mall,

and immediately behind the surviving frontage is Stourbridge Public Library. Yet the square Georgian-styled windows, the columns and the round arch of the original entrance all add up to something better than its component parts. The drawing also shows the tower of Stourbridge Town Hall soaring above the rest of the buildings in Market Street.

Although the High Street in Stourbridge has been rebuilt, it still manages to retain its human scale. In the earlier photograph Dudley & Stourbridge tramcar No 25, dating from 1901, waits in High Street at the end of the double-track section. *Commercial postcard/D. R. Harvey*

**Above and right:** Two views of the Town Clock, the Market Hall and High Street in about 1920 and April 2007 just before it was repainted. Noticeable is the different frontage of the attractively proportioned retail premises on the corner of High Street and Market Street. It has often been said that once buildings become too tall they lose their human touch, and many town redevelopments have become impersonal concrete canyons.

Originally the entrance to the Town Hall had a canopy with wrought iron pillars and framework and a frosted glass roof, but this had been demolished before this early post-war photograph of Market Street was taken. The tower of the Town Hall disproportionately dominates Market Street, suggesting that either it is too big or that the Town Hall could have been a storey taller. Although the fabric of the street today has hardly changed since the Edwardian period, until the Stourbridge Ring Road was opened, traffic along Market Street was two-way. In the distance is a late-1930s Midland Red SOS FEDD double-decker. Parked in the street on the right is a Worcestershire-registered pre-war Standard Flying Eight, while parked alongside the shops is a Vauxhall J Fourteen-Six and beyond that, outside the site of the former Falcon Inn, is a Singer Ten. Interestingly, all three cars were introduced just before the Second World War and were, unusually, re-introduced, virtually unaltered, in 1945 when car-manufacturing resumed in this country. *D. R. Harvey collection*

The second drawing depicts Stourbridge Town Hall. This red-brick building with its set of quietly dignified entrance steps is somewhat hidden in Market Street, with the tower being its only distinguishing feature. It was designed by the Stourbridge architect Thomas Robinson and completed in 1887 to commemorate Queen Victoria's Golden Jubilee at a cost of about £5,000, which was raised by public subscription. The 108-foot-long concert hall was originally able to hold around 1,000 people could also be used for dinners or political rallies, while the auditorium could be converted into a ballroom. Today the capacity of the Town Hall has been reduced to a more manageable 700. Part of the building originally contained the town's fire station, which was distinguished by having the telephone number 'Stourbridge 1', as well as containing the Council Chamber and offices.

*Right:* Back at the Town Clock, the view into Lower High Street shows one of the best-known vintners on the corner of Coventry Street, while occupying the buildings out of sight is a French restaurant and delicatessen. The buildings around the corner from Lower High Street into Coventry Street date from the 18th century and remain a delightful surviving remnant of the old town. The Yorkshire Bank on the extreme right was originally owned by the London City & Midland Bank, and was rebuilt after the Great War into this 'municipal' bank style with a typical Portland Stone frontage. *D. R. Harvey*

*Below:* Just visible further down Lower High Street is the honey brickwork of the present-day King Edward VI College. Having passed some genuinely old buildings in Lower High Street, not least the lovely 18th-century town house with its distinctive Dutch-style ogee gables, the buildings of this educational establishment are not exactly what they appear to be! Although the school dates from the 16th century, receiving its charter in 1552, the present structure can only pretend to be that old! The pretty tower and gatehouse, as well as the section of the building on the left, were built in 1862 to the Gothic design of Thomas Smith, while the Elizabethan-style building with its long transomed windows on the right of the drawing date from as late as 1908. The main entrance is now closed, as the steep, narrow steps are considered too dangerous for everyday use.

# 39.
# *Tipton and its level crossing*

Tipton is today a reviving town, having suffered terribly from the exhaustion of its local raw materials and the decline of the industries that thrived on them. Because of the location of its main street, it still looks like a town centre leading to nowhere. Owen Street, a bustling Victorian retail centre, starts immediately beyond the hump-back Brindley canal bridge over the 1772 Birmingham Canal to the south-west, and is cut short by the later Telford-built Wolverhampton Level of the Birmingham Canal. If this was not enough, at the north-easterly end of Owen Street, within yards of this canal, is the adjacent Stour Valley railway line. Within this distance of about 300 yards is the town centre of Tipton, which today is gradually recovering from many years of urban decline and decay.

In 1950 old-style gates swung over the road when rail traffic had priority, but today barriers have replaced them. On

*Above:* The drawing shows how the level crossing at Owen Street looked in about 1950, just after nationalisation and before the signal box was renamed Tipton Owen Street on 1 July of that year. The ex-LMS 'Black Five' 4-6-0 mixed-traffic locomotive, whose tender is passing over the level crossing, is pulling a London-bound express from Wolverhampton High Level towards Birmingham New Street. On the left are the station buildings dating from 1852, which in these early British Railways days still have their wooden platform canopy with the decorative valanced edges.

the remainder of the West Midlands electrified main line, only the stations at Canley, Tile Hill and Berkswell, all of which are between Birmingham and Coventry, had level crossings, and these were all removed or replaced between 2003 and 2005.

This is due to happen at Owen Street during 2008 when a multi-million-pound development is due to take place that will involve the construction of a road underpass to the east of the station at the

*Above:* It is the railway level crossing at the end of Owen Street that is the real 'gem', though for the countless number of motorists over the years who have been forced to wait as one train after another speeds, cruises or even trundles across it, the word 'gem' might be a little optimistic. With the wooden Tipton signal box behind the level crossing gates, a Midland Red bus – No 3570 (MHA 70), a Guy 'Arab' III with a Guy H30/26R body – is working on the 244 service from High Bullen in Wednesbury to Cradley Heath railway station by way of Great Bridge, Dudley, Netherton and Old Hill in about 1960.
*D. Wilson*

*Below:* Tipton level crossing remains an anachronism today, as it is still the only one on the former LNWR Stour Valley main line. Despite passing into the hands of the LMS at the Grouping in 1923, becoming part of the nationalised British Railways in 1948, seeing the demise of steam-hauled trains and, in 1966, being wired for electric traction, the level crossing remains intact. The April 2005 photograph shows a Class 323 electric multiple unit, built by Hunslet in 1992, passing on its way to Birmingham New Street from Wolverhampton. When the barriers are down pedestrians can use the underpass, which also connects the level crossing end of the up and down platforms.
*D. R. Harvey*

end of the present-day car park. Thus the level crossing is an 'about to disappear gem', much to the relief of the thousands of motorists who have waited for trains to pass and the barriers to be lifted.

Tipton was one of the cradles of the Industrial Revolution, with local supplies of coal and iron ore giving rise to the development. The problem with the area was that it was always troubled with terrible underground flooding. In fact, Thomas Newcomen's first production stationary steam pumping engine was installed at Burnt Tree, Tipton, and despite the construction of many of the later Boulton-Watt pumping engines, the ingress of water into the underground workings continued to blight the coal and iron extraction industries until these raw materials became exhausted in the 1930s. Dependent on the coal and iron deposits were the extensive 19th-century ironworks, the largest being at Horseley and Bloomfield, where iron girders, chains, cables, oven grates, rails and

bridges were produced, as well as the world's first iron steamship, the Aaron Manby, in 1821. Just as the names of the streets in Tipton, including Union Street, Canal Street, Brickkiln Street, Wood Street, Coppice Street and Factory Road, show what the growing industrial town was like, so it was that the canals in Tipton gave rise to the town being known as 'the Venice of the Midlands', a title drawn more from the Black Country sense of humour than any reality!

Just as Tipton was surrounded by two main-line canals and numerous arms and basins, the later railways were also profligate with their trackwork, sidings and marshalling yards. Tipton once had seven railway stations belonging to the LNWR and the GWR, and six goods depots, though only the station at the end of Owen Street survives today. The LNWR opened its Stour Valley line between the recently completed Birmingham New Street station and Wolverhampton on 1 July 1852. There were seven intermediate stations, including the one in Tipton, which crossed the main road by means of a level crossing, which has been at the end of Owen Street ever since.

*Left:* **Tipton's platform buildings are seen on 15 April 2005 as Central Trains EMU No 323211 pulls away from the station, with the level crossing barriers still down for what turned out to be the ninth consecutive train to pass through the station since they had been lowered some 12 minutes earlier!** *D. R. Harvey*

The view from the bridge over the original Birmingham Canal around the end of the 19th century shows the Fountain Inn in Owen Street on the corner of Factory Road. This pub, restored as recently as 1984, was the home of the famous bare-fisted prize-fighter William Perry, better known as the 'Tipton Slasher' because of his speciality punch, a slashing right-hander that in today's parlance was a swinging right hook.. He was originally a bargee who made his pugilistic reputation by fighting other bargees in order to win the right to be first to take his boat through a canal lock. Born in 1819, Perry became the Champion of England between 1850 and 1857, having earned his reputation as a hard-punching fighter over the previous 15 years. Having made a fortune, despite a gypsy's prophesy of doom, he ill-advisedly took on one Tommy Sayers in 1857 and gambled his pub in West Bromwich and his trophies, boxing belts and jewellery on his victory. Needless to say, he lost in ten rounds, and lost his fortune in the process.

The present-day view from the canal bridge towards Tipton station shows that only the Fountain Inn and St Paul's Church, which dates from 1838, have survived since the end of Queen Victoria's reign. Modern developments have helped to widen Owen Street, but have taken away whatever charm it might have had, although strangely the road alignment has remained virtually unaltered. *Commercial postcard/D. R. Harvey*

# Index